LOAN BY DESIGN

How Good Commercial Loans Are Built, Before Credit Ever Sees Them

Chad W. Maze

The Discipline of Banking™

First edition

Published by **Discipline of Banking Press**
United States of America

ISBN: 979-8-9956359-6-3 (paperback)
ISBN: 979-8-9956359-7-0 (eBook)
ISBN: 979-8-9956359-8-7 (audiobook)
Library of Congress Control Number: 2026909316

LEGAL DISCLAIMER This book is provided for informational and educational purposes only. It does not constitute legal, regulatory, accounting, tax, investment, or financial advice. The author and publisher make no representations or warranties regarding the accuracy, completeness, or applicability of the content to any specific institution, transaction, or circumstance. Readers should consult qualified professional advisors before making decisions that may affect their institution, organization, or personal financial situation. The views expressed in this book are those of the author and do not necessarily reflect the views of any employer, board, institution, regulator, or organization with which the author is or has been affiliated. References to laws, regulations, supervisory guidance, or industry practices are provided for general context only and may change over time.

Printed in the United States of America

Discipline of Banking Press is an imprint of Camino De Oro Enterprises, LLC.

Acknowledgments

This book started as a conversation I kept having.

Over the years, I found myself sitting across from bankers who were smart, well-intentioned, and genuinely trying to serve their clients, but who had never been taught how to think about commercial lending from the front end. They knew the products. They knew the policies. What they were missing was the framework underneath it all: the part that happens before the spreadsheet opens, before the credit memo is written, before the loan either works or doesn't.

This book is my attempt to give that framework a home.

To the borrowers who trusted me over the years with their businesses, their plans, and sometimes their fears, thank you. I learned more from those conversations than from any training I ever attended. The deals that went well taught me what good structure looks like. The ones that were harder taught me what I should have asked earlier. Both kinds are in this book.

To the bankers I've worked alongside, coached, and learned from, you know who you are. The good ones never stopped asking questions, even after they had every reason to assume they already knew the answers. That instinct is what this book is trying to cultivate in others.

To the credit professionals who pushed back on deals I brought them, and were right to do so, I'm grateful more than I ever said in the moment. Your questions made me better. The loans that came back with conditions taught me more about structure than the ones that sailed through.

Writing a book about something you care about is harder than it sounds, mostly because you keep finding things you should have said differently. I am indebted to the readers who looked at early drafts and were honest about what wasn't landing, what was missing, and what was taking too long to get to the point. This book is clearer because of them.

I am grateful to everyone who has ever asked me a genuine question about commercial lending, not to challenge, but to understand. Those questions reminded me that the concepts in this book aren't obvious, that they have to be taught, and that they are worth teaching carefully.

To my family, thank you for the patience. Writing happens in the margins of a full life, and the margins in our house are often crowded. Your willingness to give me time for this, and your gracious pretending not to notice when my mind was on a chapter instead of a conversation, made it possible.

And to anyone reading this who is early in their commercial lending journey: the fact that you're here, trying to understand the "why" behind the work rather than just learning the mechanics, already puts you ahead. The rest is practice, patience, and a willingness to slow down when something doesn't quite add up.

That instinct will serve you well.

Table of Contents

Prologue

The meeting is in a back booth at a diner. It's 8:15 on a Tuesday morning and the banker got there first.

The borrower, a woman named Carol who has run a dry-cleaning business for nineteen years, slides in across from him and sets a folder on the table. She's had this meeting before. She knows how it goes.

She needs $340,000. She wants to buy the building she's been leasing for eleven years. The landlord is selling. She has thirty days to decide if she wants first right of refusal.

The banker, two years out of a consumer lending role, still learning the commercial side, opens his notebook. He's prepared. He has a checklist. He starts at the top.

"What's the purchase price?"

"$340,000."

"And you're looking to finance the full amount?"

"I have about $60,000 I could put in. So $280,000."

"Okay. And the business has been operating at this location how long?"

"Eleven years. I've been here since before you were doing this job." She says it without edge. It's just true.

"Right. And revenue last year?"

"About $820,000."

He writes it down. He's moving efficiently. He asks about her tax returns, her existing debt, her current lease payment. She answers everything. She's been through this before.

Forty minutes later he tells her he'll take it to credit and let her know within the week.

Carol picks up her folder. She's not sure if that went well or not.

The banker submits the package. It comes back with a request for more information: two more years of tax returns, a personal financial statement, a copy of the current lease.

He gathers everything. Resubmits. Another week passes.

Credit comes back with a decline.

The reason: cash flow is insufficient to support the additional debt load given existing obligations. DSCR 0.94x.

The banker calls Carol. He reads her the decline language. She's quiet for a moment.

"So what does that mean?" she asks.

"It means the loan doesn't meet our coverage requirements."

Another pause.

"I've been paying $3,200 a month in rent for eleven years," she says. "The loan payment would be $2,100. How does that not work?"

He doesn't have a clean answer. He says he'll look into it.

What he discovers, when he goes back through the file, is something he should have found in the first meeting.

Carol has a $95,000 equipment line at another bank, fully drawn, that's been renewing annually for six years. She also has a personal loan, $44,000 remaining, that she took out four years ago to cover a cash shortfall during a slow stretch. Combined debt service on those two obligations plus the proposed real estate loan pushed coverage below 1.0x.

None of that was hidden. It was all in the tax returns and the personal financial statement. He had the information. He just hadn't asked the right questions to understand it.

He also hadn't asked about the equipment line. Or what the slow stretch four years ago had been about. Or whether the $60,000 she had set aside for a down payment was her only liquid reserve, or part of a larger cushion.

He'd collected data. He hadn't done discovery.

Carol lost her window on the building. The landlord sold to a developer six weeks later. Eighteen months after that, her lease wasn't renewed. She relocated, lost about 30% of her customer base in the move, and spent two years rebuilding.

None of that was inevitable.

This book is not about that banker's failure. He was competent, well-intentioned, and doing what he'd been trained to do.

It's about what he didn't know yet.

He didn't know that the first conversation with a commercial borrower isn't a qualification exercise, it's a diagnostic one. That the right questions aren't on a checklist. That the information that matters most usually doesn't arrive in response to a direct question, it surfaces when a borrower feels understood enough to offer it.

He didn't know that a loan declined by credit is almost always a loan that wasn't fully shaped at the front end. That the credit memo is the end of a process, not the beginning of one. That by the time underwriting sees a deal, most of the outcome has already been determined.

He didn't know that Carol's deal probably had a path, a structure that addressed the coverage problem, right-sized the down payment, refinanced the equipment line, and built a case credit could say yes to. He didn't know how to find it. Nobody had taught him.

That's what this book is for.

What a Different Conversation Looks Like

Imagine the same diner. Same booth. Same Carol, same folder, same thirty-day window.

A different banker sits across from her.

She starts the same way: she needs $340,000, she has $60,000, she wants to buy the building.

The banker writes it down. Then she sets her pen aside.

"Before we get into the numbers, tell me about the business. You've been here eleven years. Walk me through how a typical week runs."

Carol talks. She explains the operation: drop-offs peak Tuesday through Thursday, pickup Friday and Saturday, Mondays are slow. The equipment runs constantly in season, less so in winter. She has three employees, two of them full-time. Her biggest costs are labor, utilities, and chemical supplies.

"And financially, what does a good month look like versus a slow one?"

Carol thinks about it. Good month, maybe $78,000 in revenue. January and February are slow, closer to $51,000. The fixed costs don't move much. January is always a little uncomfortable.

"That's useful. I want to ask about a couple of other things, not to be nosy, but because it'll affect how I build this. Do you have any other debt on the business right now? Anything at other banks?"

Carol tells her about the equipment line. Fully drawn, has been for a while. Renews every year. She'd been meaning to address it but it keeps getting deferred.

"And the $60,000 for the down payment, is that your full liquid reserve, or is there more behind it?"

It's most of it, Carol admits. She has another $18,000 in a personal account she'd rather not touch.

The banker nods. She's not writing faster. She's thinking.

"Here's what I'm seeing," she says. "The building makes sense for you. You're paying $3,200 a month in rent and the loan payment would be less. That math works. But there are a couple of things I want to solve before we build the structure, because if we don't, it'll come back from credit and we'll have lost your window."

She explains: the equipment line, fully drawn and renewing annually, is carrying risk the structure needs to address. And putting $60,000 down depletes the operating reserve below what she'd want to see. She has two ideas.

First: can they refinance the equipment line into a clean term loan alongside the real estate? It would raise the total borrowing slightly but eliminate a revolving obligation that credit will flag.

Second: rather than putting $60,000 down and having almost nothing left, what if they structured the deal with $45,000 down and kept $15,000 in reserve? The loan is slightly larger, but Carol goes into ownership with a cushion instead of without one. Especially with January coming.

Carol looks at her.

"You're the first banker who's ever explained the whole picture to me before submitting anything."

The deal structured differently goes to credit with the equipment line refinanced, right-sized down payment, and coverage addressed. It's approved. Carol buys her building.

Two years later she refinances into better terms. The relationship is still active.

The difference between those two conversations isn't talent. It isn't experience, exactly, though experience helps. It's a framework, a way of approaching the front end of a commercial deal that surfaces what matters before the loan is built rather than after it's declined.

That framework is what this book is about.

It starts at the front end, with the conversation, the discovery, the questions most bankers don't know to ask yet. And it ends with a way of thinking about commercial lending that you can carry into every deal you touch from here.

Carol's story doesn't have to end the way it did.

Neither does the next one.

How to Use This Book

This book is meant to be used, not just read.

If you're coming from consumer or branch banking, you already know more than you think. You know how to listen to people, assess risk, and make responsible decisions under pressure. That's not nothing. That's actually most of the job.

Commercial lending just asks you to apply those instincts differently.

In consumer lending, the product already exists. Your job is to find the right fit. In commercial lending, there is no preset product. The loan has to be built, shaped around a specific business, a specific need, and a specific moment in time. That shift from *matching* to *building* is what this book is about.

What This Book Is (and Isn't)

Let's be clear about what you're holding.

This is not a credit policy manual. It won't walk you through underwriting models, debt service calculations, or loan committee procedures. There are good resources for that, and your credit team exists for a reason.

What this book *is* is something harder to find: a guide to how experienced commercial lenders actually think. The questions they ask before the spreadsheet opens. The patterns they recognize before a deal goes sideways. The language they use to help a borrower understand why structure matters, without making it feel like a lecture.

Think of it as the front end of the job. The part that happens in conversations, in discovery, in the quiet work of shaping a request into something that makes sense. Most outcomes in commercial lending are decided here, long before credit ever sees the file.

Who This Book Is For

This book is written for you if you're making the move from consumer or branch banking into business or commercial lending, or if you're already there and want to feel more confident in the work.

You don't need a credit background to benefit from it. You need to be curious about *why* loans work, not just whether they get approved.

It's also useful if you're a branch manager supporting business customers, a business development officer early in your commercial career, or anyone who understands products but wants to understand structure.

If you've ever left a borrower conversation thinking *something felt off but I couldn't explain what*, this book is especially for you.

How the Book Is Organized

The book follows the same path a well-built commercial loan does: from the front end forward.

The early chapters focus on mindset, how commercial lending differs from what you already know, and what separates a good loan from a good story. The middle chapters get practical: how loans are shaped, how lines and term loans actually work, and what the moving parts of structure are really doing. The later chapters bring it to life with real deal patterns, the borrower's perspective, and early warning signs to watch for. The final chapter ties it together into a way of thinking you can carry into any commercial conversation.

You don't have to read it cover to cover, though it rewards that approach. Each chapter stands on its own.

Three Ways to Use It

If you're new to commercial lending: Start at page one. The ideas build on each other, and by the time you reach the end, the shift from product thinking to structure thinking will feel natural, not foreign.

If you're learning on the job: Use it situationally. Before shaping a deal, pull up the structure chapters. When something feels familiar but off, go to the deal patterns. When you're uneasy and can't say why, read the warning signs.

When you're in the middle of a conversation: Use the reference pages. They're intentionally short and plain-language. Print them, keep them open, share them with your team. They're the distilled version of everything in the book, designed to be useful in real time, not just in training.

A Note on the Transition Itself

There is something nobody tells you about moving into commercial lending from a consumer or branch role.
For a period of time, sometimes weeks, sometimes months, you will feel less capable than you were. Not less intelligent. Not less hardworking. Less *competent.* The confidence you built over years in your previous role doesn't transfer automatically. You will sit in conversations where experienced commercial lenders seem to see things you can't see yet. You will leave client meetings unsure whether you asked the right questions. You will submit deals and wonder, not quite confidently, whether they were shaped correctly.

This is normal. It is not a sign that you're in the wrong role.

Every banker who has made this transition has gone through a version of it. The ones who succeed are not the ones who avoided the discomfort, they're the ones who stayed with it long enough for the pattern recognition to develop. Commercial lending is a craft, and crafts take time to internalize. The framework can be taught. The judgment it produces takes repetition.

> ***The goal of this book is not to make the transition feel easy. It's to make the discomfort productive, to give the uncertainty somewhere to go.***

When you don't know how to structure a deal yet, that's a normal stage of learning. When you can't explain why a loan feels off, that's pattern recognition still forming. When credit pushes back and you're not sure how to respond, that's judgment not yet built.

None of that means you aren't becoming the banker you're trying to become. It means you're in the middle of it.

The bankers who struggle most in this transition are usually not the ones who feel uncertain, they're the ones who hide it. Who say yes when they mean maybe. Who submit deals they're not sure about rather than ask a clarifying question. Who treat the discomfort as something to manage rather than something to use.

This book is an invitation to do the opposite. To ask the question you're not sure you should ask. To slow down when something feels off even if you can't name it. To treat uncertainty as the starting point for good thinking rather than evidence that you shouldn't be in the room.

You belong in the room. You're just not done yet.

None of us are.

One More Thing

This book isn't trying to replace your credit team or your institution's policies. It's trying to make your interactions with both of them better.

When you frame deals clearly, acknowledge risk honestly, and arrive at credit with the right questions already answered, those conversations stop feeling like hurdles. They start feeling collaborative.

That's the goal. And it starts at the front end, which is exactly where we're going to begin.

LOAN BY DESIGN™

PART I
FOUNDATIONS

What a good loan really is, who is really borrowing, and why structure is the banker's real product.

Structure begins at the front end, before the credit memo, before underwriting, before the first number is run. The three chapters in this part establish the foundation that everything else in this book builds on.

Chapter 1 defines what a good commercial loan actually is and why banks build them rather than find them. Chapter 2 explains who is really borrowing, the business, not the owner, and how operating cycles create the borrowing needs that drive every commercial conversation. Chapter 3 makes the case that structure is the banker's real product: the discipline that separates a well-built loan from a well-intentioned one.

Read this part before the tools. The tools only work when the foundation is in place.

CHAPTER 1

What Makes a Good Commercial Loan

A Word on Discomfort

Commercial lending is inherently ambiguous. There are no clean formulas that tell you, with certainty, whether a deal is right. The work relies on judgment, pattern recognition, and the discipline to slow down when something doesn't quite add up.

If a chapter makes you pause, that's a good sign. It means you're thinking rather than reacting.

When something feels uncomfortable, the useful question isn't whether the feeling should be ignored, it's where it's coming from. Is the discomfort a signal of risk, or simply the unease of unfamiliar territory? Learning to tell the difference is a core front-end skill. This book is designed to help you develop it.

Weak front-end structure rarely shows up as immediate loss. Instead, it creates noise, renewals that feel harder than they should, exceptions that quietly accumulate, restructures that feel necessary but never quite satisfying. Over time, institutions respond to that noise by tightening policy, adding controls, and slowing decision-making.

This book exists to prevent that quiet degradation.

Most people think banks make loans by saying "yes" or "no."

Good commercial lenders know that's wrong.

Banks don't *find* good loans. They *build* them.

This distinction sounds small. It isn't. It's the difference between a banker who matches borrowers to products and one who shapes risk into something that actually works, for the borrower and the bank. Everything in this chapter flows from that idea.

A Good Loan Is Not the Same Thing as a Good Business

This is the first mindset shift, and for many bankers coming from consumer roles, it's the most disorienting one.

A business can have great people, a strong reputation, a compelling story, and growing revenue, and still be a poor credit. This happens more often than you'd expect.

The reason is simple: banks don't lend to stories. Banks lend to **repayment**.

A good commercial loan stands on its own, even if the business hits a rough patch, even if growth slows, even if the owner gets distracted. The structure of a good loan anticipates stress instead of hoping it never arrives.

When experienced lenders talk about "credit quality," they're not talking about how impressive the borrower is. They're asking whether the loan makes sense under normal conditions *and* under pressure.

What Banks Actually Lend Against

Here's the most important truth in commercial lending, and it's worth saying plainly:

> ***Banks lend against cash flow. Everything else is support.***

Not ideas. Not collateral. Not guarantees. Cash flow is the primary source of repayment, full stop.

When a business borrows money, the loan gets repaid by customers paying invoices, products being sold, services being delivered, and revenue turning into cash. That's the mechanism. Everything else in the deal exists to protect the bank if that mechanism breaks down.

Collateral exists to reduce loss *if* repayment fails. Guarantees exist to keep owners aligned *if* things get uncomfortable. Neither one replaces a weak cash flow story.

If you remember nothing else from this chapter, remember this: if a loan only works because of collateral or a guarantor, it doesn't really work.

The Three Questions Every Good Loan Answers

Before structure, before terms, before credit approval, every good commercial loan has clear, plain-language answers to three questions. If those answers are vague, or missing, the loan probably isn't ready.

1. Why is the borrower borrowing?

"Growth" is not an answer. "Opportunity" is not an answer. "Because they qualify" is definitely not an answer.

A good loan starts with a specific business purpose: buying equipment that increases capacity, financing inventory ahead of a busy season, smoothing cash flow between expenses and collections, purchasing owner-occupied real estate, or funding an acquisition with a clear integration plan.

The reason matters because it drives everything else, loan type, term, structure, and risk profile. When purpose is vague, structure becomes vague. And vague structure is where problems begin.

A useful test: can you explain the use of proceeds in one sentence that a nonbanker would understand? If not, it probably isn't simple enough yet.

2. How will the loan be repaid?

This is the heart of commercial credit thinking, and it's where consumer lending instincts often fall short.

In consumer lending, repayment comes from personal income. In commercial lending, it comes from business cash flow. That distinction changes everything.

A strong repayment story explains where the cash comes from, when it comes in, why it's reliable, and how it covers the debt over time. It does *not* rely on asset liquidation, owner bailouts, or best-case scenarios.

Experienced lenders are not pessimists, but they are realistic. They expect variability. They assume friction. They plan for delays. A good loan works without heroic assumptions.

3. What happens if things don't go as planned?

This is where structure earns its keep.

Every loan should be able to answer: what if revenue dips? What if expenses rise? What if growth stalls? What if the owner loses focus?

A good loan doesn't pretend those things won't happen. It's built so that *if* they do, the bank has options and the borrower has incentives to address problems early. This is why terms, collateral, guarantees, and covenants exist, not to punish borrowers, but to create early warning and shared accountability.

Good loans don't avoid risk. They manage it.

Borrower vs. Guarantor: A Critical Distinction

At the front end of lending, one of the most common misunderstandings is the role of the guarantor. It's worth being direct about this.

The **borrower** is the business entity. It generates revenue, pays expenses, produces cash flow, and repays the loan. This is where the loan lives or dies.

The **guarantor** is usually an owner. Their role is to backstop behavior, stay engaged, and share downside risk. A guarantor is not the repayment plan.

Strong guarantors improve otherwise sound loans. They do not rescue weak ones.

When you hear a deal described as "okay because the guarantor is strong," treat that as a warning sign, not a comfort. A good commercial loan works without relying on the guarantor. The guarantor exists to make sure everyone stays aligned.

The Quiet Importance of Timing

Timing doesn't get enough attention at the front end of lending, but it matters more than many ratios.

The same business can be too early for bank credit, perfectly bankable, or too late and already stressed, depending entirely on when you meet them. Good timing looks like stable operations, predictable cash flow, and a clear next step that isn't a desperate one.

Bad timing often sounds like: "This loan will fix everything." Or: "We just need a little runway." Or: "Once this one thing happens..."

Banks are not turnaround specialists. They are partners in *ongoing* businesses. A good loan meets a business where it is, not where it hopes to be.

The Banker's Real Job

At the front end of commercial lending, your job is not to approve loans.

Your job is to ask better questions, clarify the story, identify risk early, and shape requests into structures that make sense. You are helping turn raw opportunity into something credit-ready.

That's not salesmanship. That's craftsmanship.

When done well, the credit conversation becomes a confirmation, not a confrontation.

The Standard to Hold Yourself To

Here's a simple test you can apply to any commercial loan at the front end:

> ***If this loan were already on the books, would I feel comfortable explaining it to someone else six months from now, without making excuses?***

Good loans age well. Bad loans feel uncomfortable almost immediately.

This book is about helping you recognize the difference, before the loan ever exists.

In the next chapter, we'll take the next step: understanding who is actually borrowing, how businesses create borrowing needs, and why commercial lending starts with the operating cycle, not the balance sheet.

CHAPTER 2

Who Is Really Borrowing, and Why That Matters

At the front end of commercial lending, one of the most common mistakes is answering the wrong question.

The question isn't: "Who wants the loan?"

The real question is: "Who is actually borrowing, and how do they produce repayment?"

Get that wrong, and everything that follows, structure, terms, guarantees, even SBA, gets built on a shaky foundation. This chapter is about learning to see borrowers clearly: separating the person from the business and understanding how borrowing needs are actually created.

The Borrower Is the Business, Not the Owner

This sounds obvious. It's surprisingly easy to forget, especially for bankers coming from consumer or branch roles, where the person in front of you *is* the borrower.

In commercial lending, the borrower is the legal business entity. The business generates cash flow. The business repays the loan. Owners matter, but they are not the borrower.

A business can be well-run, profitable, and growing, and still be structurally misaligned with a particular loan request. The reverse is also true: a modest, unglamorous business can be an excellent credit because its cash flow is steady, its needs are well-defined, and its structure fits.

That's why commercial lending starts with understanding **how the business works**, not how impressive the owner is.

How Businesses Create Borrowing Needs

Businesses don't borrow money because they feel like it. They borrow because cash moves through the business unevenly.

Every operating business lives inside a cycle: spend money, do work or produce goods, get paid later. That gap, between when money goes out and when it comes back, is where borrowing lives.

> ***The operating cycle is the most important concept in front-end commercial lending.***

Most businesses follow some version of this pattern: cash goes out to pay employees, suppliers, and rent; work is performed or goods are sold; invoices are issued; cash eventually comes back in. The longer that cycle is, the more financing pressure the business feels.

Good lenders don't just ask how much a business wants to borrow. They ask where in the cycle the pressure is occurring. That's the question that leads to the right structure.

Different Businesses, Different Cycles

Two businesses can have identical revenue and very different borrowing needs. Consider:

- A retail store collects cash immediately but must buy inventory upfront
- A contractor pays labor weekly but may not get paid for 60–90 days
- A manufacturer buys raw materials months before selling finished goods
- A professional services firm may have minimal assets but uneven billing cycles

Each of these businesses experiences cash flow stress differently, and that stress determines what kind of loan structure actually makes sense.

This is why front-end discovery matters more than product knowledge. You can't match the right structure to the wrong problem. And you can't understand the problem without understanding how cash actually moves.

Why "How Much Do You Need?" Is the Wrong First Question

When a borrower names a specific dollar amount early in a conversation, it's tempting to anchor on that number. That's a mistake.

The better first question is: *"What problem are you trying to solve?"*

Loan amounts should come from operating needs, asset costs, timing gaps, and repayment capacity, not from the borrower's opening ask. When the amount is guessed first and justified later, loans tend to be oversized, become permanent, and create stress instead of relief.

Good lenders size loans to the **problem**, not the optimism.

The Business Makes the Payments

A commercial borrower doesn't "make payments." The **business** makes payments. That distinction matters more than it sounds.

Businesses fluctuate. Revenue is uneven. Expenses don't wait. Customers pay late. These aren't underwriting details yet, they're structural signals. They tell you whether a loan should be short or long, flexible or fixed, revolving or amortizing.

At the front end, you should always be listening for seasonality, customer concentration, dependency on key relationships, and sensitivity to labor or input costs. These patterns shape the loan before the numbers ever come in.

Owners Matter: But Differently Than You Think

Owners are critical in commercial lending, but not for the reason most people assume.

Owners matter because they control decisions, influence risk, and determine how a business behaves under stress. They do *not* matter because they're a backup paycheck.

When owners describe their business, listen carefully. How do they explain challenges? Do they understand their own cash flow? How do they describe past problems, do they take responsibility or assign blame?

These signals tell you how a borrower will behave *after* the loan is made. That matters far more than how they behave during the pitch.

Borrower vs. Guarantor: Keeping the Roles Straight

It's worth revisiting this distinction from the front-end perspective, because it's where a lot of deals go sideways.

The **borrower** is the business entity, the source of repayment and the focus of structure. The **guarantor** is (usually) the owner, the alignment mechanism, the accountability layer.

Guarantees exist to keep borrowers engaged when things get uncomfortable. They don't turn bad loans into good ones.

If a deal sounds safe *only* because the guarantor is wealthy, pause. That's not comfort, that's a warning sign dressed up as reassurance.

Why Bankers Get This Wrong

Most front-end mistakes aren't made out of carelessness. They happen because of incomplete framing.

Bankers focus on the person instead of the business. They jump to products before understanding the problem. They treat guarantees as solutions. They skip over the operating cycle because no one told them it mattered.

Once you learn to see the borrower as a **cash flow system**, lending conversations change immediately. You stop selling. You start diagnosing.

The Banker's Advantage

Bankers often see things credit never will: early growth signals, emerging stress, informal practices, real-world behavior that doesn't show up in financial statements.

Your job isn't to turn those observations into conclusions. Your job is to turn them into better structure.

That starts by understanding who is really borrowing, why they need funds, and how cash actually moves through the business. Everything else builds from there.

A Simple Test

Before moving forward with any commercial opportunity, ask yourself:

> ***If this business stopped growing tomorrow, would the loan still make sense?***

If the answer is no, the issue isn't growth. It's structure.

And structure, how to build it, size it, and align it with the real needs of a real business, is exactly what the next chapter is about.

In the next chapter, we'll move from understanding the borrower to understanding the lender's craft: how loan structure turns business risk into something a bank can say yes to, and how good structure solves more problems than perfect credit ever will.

CHAPTER 3

Structure Is the Banker's Real Product

Most borrowers think banks sell money.

Most new bankers think banks sell loan products.

Experienced commercial lenders know something different:

> ***Banks don't sell money. Banks sell structure.***

Money is a commodity. Any bank can provide it. Structure is the craft, and it's where the real work happens.

Two banks can lend the same amount, to the same borrower, at roughly the same rate, and produce very different outcomes based on how the loan is structured. One performs quietly for years. The other becomes a problem almost immediately. The difference is rarely credit policy. It's structure.

What "Structure" Really Means

At the front end, structure isn't legal language or documentation. It's the way risk is translated into something manageable.

Loan structure answers one essential question:

> ***How does this loan get repaid over time, and what happens if it doesn't go exactly as planned?***

Everything else flows from that. When lenders talk about structure, they're talking about how amount, term, amortization, repayment source, collateral, guarantees, and monitoring all fit together. Each element does a specific job. When they're aligned, risk becomes manageable. When they're not, even strong borrowers feel the pressure.

Why Structure Matters More Than Credit Quality

This may sound uncomfortable, but it's worth saying directly:

> ***Strong borrowers can carry weak structure. Weak borrowers cannot.***

Good structure can reduce risk, absorb volatility, create early warnings, and give everyone time to react. Poor structure magnifies problems, even for otherwise solid businesses.

That's why experienced lenders focus less on whether a borrower is "good" and more on whether the loan **fits** the business. A well-fitting loan is one that works in normal months and survives difficult ones.

Your Job Is to Shape Requests, Not Approve Them

At the front end, your job is not to approve loans. Your job is to shape requests into something approvable.

That means right-sizing the amount, matching the term to the asset or need, aligning repayment with cash flow, identifying risk before credit does, and adjusting structure instead of forcing decisions.

A well-structured loan often moves smoothly through credit because most of the hard thinking has already been done. When credit pushes back, it's usually because something at the front end wasn't fully resolved. That's feedback, not obstruction.

The Three Core Structural Questions

Before any deal goes to credit, a good banker should be able to answer three questions clearly and in plain language.

1. What is the loan actually for?

Structure starts with purpose. Loans work best when the use of proceeds is narrow, the benefit is measurable, and the timeline is realistic.

Problems arise when loans try to do too many things at once: cover operating losses, fund growth, refinance old problems, and buy time. That's not structure, that's hope bundled into a single request. Good structure separates needs and addresses them individually.

2. How does repayment match the business?

Repayment should follow cash flow, not convenience.

This is where many front-end mistakes happen: long-term needs funded short-term, short-term needs locked into long amortizations, revolving needs placed into term loans, permanent debt disguised as temporary financing.

Good structure asks: when does cash come in, how predictable is it, and what happens during slow periods? Loans should breathe with the business, not fight it.

3. What protects the bank if reality deviates?

Reality always deviates. Good structure assumes delays, cost overruns, customer issues, and management distractions, not because failure is expected, but because resilience has to be built in.

Protection comes from appropriate collateral, guarantees that align incentives, and terms that force a review before problems grow too large. This isn't about being defensive. It's about being realistic.

Structure Is Where Creativity Lives

One of the most misunderstood ideas in commercial lending is creativity. Creativity is not bending rules. It's problem-solving within discipline.

Examples of front-end structural creativity:

- Reducing the loan amount instead of declining the deal
- Splitting one request into a line and a term loan
- Shortening amortization but extending maturity
- Using SBA to solve structure gaps, not credit gaps
- Phasing financing instead of funding everything upfront

Good structure often comes from asking: *"What's the cleanest version of this deal that still solves the problem?"*

Why Bad Structure Feels Fine at First

Poorly structured loans rarely look bad on day one. They look bad at six months, at twelve months, at the first unexpected slowdown.

You've probably heard the warning signs before, even if you didn't recognize them as such: "They'll refinance later." "This will clean itself up." "Next year will be better." "We can always restructure."

Each of those phrases is a signal that structure isn't doing its job. Strong structure reduces the need for rescue later. That's the point.

Products Don't Matter Until Structure Is Clear

Many front-end conversations jump too quickly to products: line of credit, term loan, SBA, real estate loan. That's backwards.

Products are just containers. Structure is what goes inside them.

A line of credit with the wrong size or purpose is worse than no line at all. A term loan with the wrong amortization creates stress instead of relief. The product can't fix a structural mismatch, it can only make it more official.

Start with structure. Products follow naturally.

The Banker's Advantage

Credit teams see deals at a moment in time. Bankers see the evolution of the business, the real motivations behind requests, the early signs of strain or growth, how borrowers behave before money is involved.

That perspective is invaluable, but only if it gets translated into structure. Your role is not to argue for approval. Your role is to deliver a deal that makes sense, one that credit can look at and immediately understand.

A Simple Structural Discipline

Before sending any deal forward, ask yourself:

> ***If this loan were already outstanding, what would worry me six months from now?***

Then fix that, with structure.

That's the work. That's the craft. That's the banker's real product.

In the next chapter, we'll get more concrete: the major building blocks of commercial loan structure, amount, term, amortization, collateral, and guarantees, and how each one changes risk long before underwriting ever gets involved.

PART II
BUILDING BLOCKS

The elements, instruments, and tools that determine how a loan actually works.

Every commercial loan, regardless of type, size, or industry, is assembled from the same set of building blocks. This part explains what those blocks are, how they interact, and how adjusting one changes everything else.

Chapter 4 introduces the seven structural elements and how each one shapes risk. Chapter 5 distinguishes lines from term loans and explains when each instrument actually fits. Chapter 6 covers SBA as a structuring tool, not a fallback. Chapter 7 addresses pricing and rate, what they are, how they're determined, and why a banker who understands structure never competes on basis points. Chapter 8 explains general terms: what they mean, why they exist, and how to use them honestly.

By the end of this part, a banker can look at any commercial request and understand not just what product might apply, but why the structure should be built the way it should.

CHAPTER 4

The Building Blocks of Loan Structure

Once you understand that structure is the banker's real product, the next step is learning what structure is actually made of.

Commercial loan structure isn't complicated, but it is precise. Each element exists for a reason. When those elements align with the business, loans work quietly in the background. When they don't, even strong borrowers feel the pressure.

Think of structure like a set of levers. You don't pull them all at once. You pull the ones that solve the problem without creating a new one. And when you adjust one, the others shift too.

This chapter walks through each building block from a front-end perspective: what it does, why it matters, and how it changes risk.

The Seven Building Blocks

Every commercial loan, no matter how simple or complex, is built from the same basic components:

- Amount
- Term
- Amortization
- Repayment source
- Collateral
- Guarantees
- Monitoring and review

None of these elements works in isolation. Together, they define how risk is distributed, who carries it, and what happens when reality doesn't go exactly as planned.

1. Loan Amount: Smaller Is Often Stronger

Loan amount is where most structure problems begin. Borrowers usually ask for what they want, what they think the bank will give, or what feels safe. None of those is the right starting point.

Good structure starts with what the business actually needs, what the cash flow can support, and what solves the problem cleanly.

Oversized loans carry hidden risk. Excess cash loses discipline. Temporary needs become permanent. Repayment starts to feel optional instead of necessary. Undersized loans create a different problem: borrowers return too quickly, pressure builds elsewhere, and confidence erodes on both sides.

> ***A well-sized loan feels boring. That's a compliment.***

A useful front-end test: if the borrower received less than this amount, would the business still function? If yes, the request may be oversized.

2. Term: How Long the Bank Is Exposed

Term answers one simple question: how long is the bank at risk?

Term should match the life of the asset, the duration of the need, and the predictability of cash flow. The most common front-end mismatches are short-term needs funded long-term, long-term assets funded short-term, and "temporary" loans with no clear exit.

Shorter terms reduce uncertainty, force review, and increase discipline. Longer terms improve cash flow and reduce payment pressure, but increase the bank's exposure to change over time.

There's no perfect term, only an appropriate one. Good structure uses term intentionally, not conveniently.

3. Amortization: How Repayment Actually Happens

Amortization is where structure becomes real. It determines payment size, the speed of principal reduction, and whether debt naturally shrinks over time.

Faster amortization reduces risk but increases payment strain. Slower amortization improves monthly cash flow but increases the bank's exposure, and can mask problems that faster repayment would have surfaced.

A common front-end mistake is assuming lower payments always help borrowers. Sometimes they don't. Long amortizations can delay discipline and create false comfort. Shorter amortization forces a business to prove it can carry debt, not just qualify for it.

Good structure balances sustainability with accountability.

4. Repayment Source: The Anchor of the Entire Deal

> ***Every loan should have a clearly identified primary source of repayment. If that sentence is fuzzy, the structure is too.***

The primary source is almost always operating cash flow, the revenue generated by customers paying invoices, products being sold, services being delivered. Secondary sources (asset liquidation, guarantees, refinancing) exist only if the primary fails.

If repayment depends on refinancing, the structure is incomplete. A lender should be able to say: "This loan gets repaid from *this* activity, over *this* timeframe, under *these* conditions." If that sentence requires significant qualification, there's more work to do.

5. Collateral: Protection, Not Permission

Collateral is one of the most misunderstood elements of structure. It reduces loss severity, provides leverage in workouts, and encourages borrower engagement. What it does *not* do is create repayment, fix cash flow problems, or turn bad deals into good ones.

Strong collateral should make lenders more comfortable, not careless.

At the front end, the right questions around collateral are: Is this collateral logically connected to the loan? Does its value persist over time? Can it realistically be accessed if needed?

Collateral that only works on paper doesn't really work.

6. Guarantees: Aligning Behavior, Not Replacing Structure

Guarantees exist because people matter. They keep owners invested, reduce moral hazard, and improve decision-making under stress. But they are not structural substitutes.

A loan that only works because of a guarantor is a loan waiting for a problem.

Guarantees strengthen good structure. They do not justify weak structure. They should never be the primary repayment plan. When guarantees are doing too much work, something more fundamental is missing, and that's what needs to be fixed.

7. Monitoring and Review: Structure's Quiet Partner

Monitoring isn't about control. It's about awareness.

Good structure builds in natural review points, required information flow, and opportunities to adjust early. This might look like annual renewals, periodic financial updates, or covenant-driven conversations.

At the front end, the goal isn't to design monitoring mechanics, it's to recognize when a deal needs them. Stable businesses need less structure. Volatile businesses need more. Ignoring that reality doesn't make risk disappear.

How the Pieces Work Together

> ***You don't fix structure by changing one thing in isolation.***

Structure is a system. When you increase the amount, you may need a shorter term. When you lengthen the term, you may need stronger collateral. When you loosen amortization, you may need tighter monitoring. When you reduce guarantees, you need better cash flow coverage.

Good bankers think in combinations, not silos. Every adjustment to one lever asks a question of the others.

Why Credit Focuses on Structure So Much

Credit teams don't obsess over structure because they're rigid. They do it because structure determines outcomes.

Numbers change. Behavior fluctuates. Markets shift. Structure remains. A well-structured loan can survive mediocre performance. A poorly structured loan cannot survive reality. That's not pessimism, it's experience.

A Front-End Discipline to Practice

Before moving a deal forward, ask yourself: which structural element is doing the hardest work in this loan?

If the answer is collateral, guarantees, or optimism, go back and rebalance. Good loans don't rely on one element to carry the weight. They distribute risk thoughtfully across all seven building blocks.

You don't need to be an underwriter to understand structure. You need to be curious, disciplined, and honest about risk. That's where bankers create the most value, and prevent the most problems.

In the next chapter, we'll put structure into action by walking through the major loan forms, lines of credit, term loans, and combinations, and when each one actually fits the business instead of forcing the business to fit the loan.

CHAPTER 5

Lines, Terms, and When to Use Each

Once bankers understand structure, the next mistake they tend to make is falling in love with products.

Lines of credit. Term loans. Real estate loans. These are not strategies, they're containers. A container only works if it matches what you're trying to carry.

This chapter is about learning when a line makes sense, when a term makes sense, when a combination makes sense, and when none of them do yet.

Start With the Problem, Not the Product

Borrowers often arrive asking for a specific loan type. That doesn't mean they're wrong, but it does mean they're starting from their perspective, not the bank's.

Bankers should reverse the order. Before reaching for a product, ask: what problem is the business trying to solve? Where is the cash pressure? How long does that pressure last? Does it repeat?

Only then does the right structure become obvious.

> ***When products are chosen first, structure gets forced. When structure comes first, products fall into place.***

Lines of Credit: Funding the Operating Cycle

A line of credit is designed to solve one problem: timing.

Lines exist to bridge the gap between when cash goes out and when it comes back in. They're best suited for inventory purchases, accounts receivable gaps, seasonal fluctuations, and short-term working capital needs. In a healthy business, a line goes up and down, self-liquidates, and supports normal operations without becoming a permanent fixture.

The key word is *temporary*.

When a Line Works Well

A line of credit makes sense when the business has recurring cycles, cash flow is predictable even if uneven, borrowings are short-lived, and there's a clear reason balances should decline.

The best front-end signal is a borrower who describes their use naturally: "We borrow, we collect, we pay it down, and then we repeat." That's a line doing its job.

When a Line Becomes a Problem

Lines create risk when they stay fully drawn, fund long-term needs, mask structural cash flow issues, or quietly replace profitability. A permanently drawn line is no longer a line, it's a term loan pretending to be flexible.

Front-end warning phrases to listen for: "We've always been fully utilized." "We need the line just in case." "It never really pays down, but it's stable."

Stability is not the same as health. When lines stop revolving, structure needs to change.

Term Loans: Financing Something with a Life

Term loans exist for one reason: to finance something that lasts longer than one operating cycle.

They're best suited for equipment, vehicles, build-outs, acquisitions, buyouts, and long-term investments. What defines a good term loan isn't the interest rate, it's alignment. The loan should match what it's financing in duration, repayment, and risk.

When a Term Loan Works Well

Term loans work when the asset or benefit has a measurable life, cash flow can support amortization, the loan naturally shrinks over time, and repayment builds equity or stability.

A good term loan feels disciplined but manageable. It should require effort, but not stress.

When a Term Loan Is Misused

Term loans create problems when they fund operating losses, replace working capital, or rely on refinancing for repayment. "This will give us breathing room" and "once things improve, we'll refinance" are phrases that should slow a banker down, not speed them up.

If repayment depends on improvement, the structure isn't finished.

Real Estate Loans: Long-Lived Assets, Long-Lived Risk

Owner-occupied real estate often feels safer than it is. Yes, real estate is tangible, has a long life, and often appreciates. But it also reduces flexibility, ties up capital, and increases fixed costs.

Real estate loans work best when the business is stable, cash flow is predictable, and ownership genuinely strengthens long-term positioning. They work poorly when real estate becomes a solution to operating problems.

> ***Real estate should support the business, not rescue it.***

Combinations: Where Front-End Craft Shows Up

Many of the best commercial loans aren't one product, they're combinations.

A line for working capital paired with a term loan for equipment. A real estate loan alongside a smaller operating line. A term loan that replaces permanent line usage and forces discipline the revolving structure never could.

Combination structures work when each piece has a clear purpose, repayment sources are distinct, and the overall structure reduces pressure instead of spreading it.

This is where bankers create real value, by separating needs instead of forcing one loan to do everything.

SBA as a Structuring Tool, Not a Product

From a front-end view, SBA is not about approval, it's about fit.

SBA often makes sense when conventional structure is too tight, amortization needs to be longer, down payment constraints exist, or risk needs to be shared more broadly. Used well, SBA solves structural mismatches. Used poorly, it justifies weak fundamentals.

A good SBA deal still follows the same rules as any other: clear purpose, real repayment, appropriate structure. SBA expands options, it doesn't change the basics of credit.

A Simple Framework for Choosing

Instead of asking "which loan do they want?", ask four questions:

- Is the need **temporary or permanent**?
- Does it **repeat or resolve**?
- Does it follow the **operating cycle or asset life**?
- Will repayment come from **operations or time**?

Lines solve cycles. Terms solve longevity. Combinations solve complexity. When the answer to those four questions is clear, the right structure becomes obvious.

The Most Common Front-End Mistake

The most common mistake is trying to make one loan solve every problem.

That usually leads to oversized facilities, permanent debt, weak discipline, and eventual restructuring. Good structure simplifies. It breaks problems apart and addresses them honestly, even when that means telling a borrower their request needs to be split, resized, or sequenced differently.

A Final Front-End Test

Before moving forward with any structure, ask:

> ***If this loan were already outstanding, would it naturally improve the business, or merely postpone decisions?***

If the answer is "postpone," the structure isn't finished yet.

Understanding lines and terms isn't about memorizing rules. It's about recognizing patterns: cash timing vs. asset life, flexibility vs. discipline, short-term relief vs. long-term health. Bankers who get this right don't just move deals forward, they make them better.

In the next chapter, we'll dig into one of the most misunderstood parts of lending: general terms, what they really mean, why they exist, and how to explain them without turning borrowers off or scaring yourself.

CHAPTER 6

SBA as a Structuring Tool

SBA gets mentioned in a lot of banking conversations. It gets understood in far fewer of them.

For many bankers coming from consumer or branch roles, SBA feels like a separate world, its own rules, its own paperwork, its own approval process. Something specialists handle. Something you reach for when a conventional deal doesn't quite work and you're not sure what else to do.

That framing isn't wrong, exactly. But it misses what SBA actually is at the front end of a deal.

> ***SBA is not a product category. It's a set of structural tools that solve specific mismatches between what a good business needs and what conventional lending can comfortably provide.***

This chapter is about understanding those mismatches, and knowing when SBA solves them, when it doesn't, and how to have an honest front-end conversation about both.

What SBA Actually Does

The SBA, the Small Business Administration, doesn't lend money directly. It guarantees a portion of loans made by approved lenders, which reduces the bank's risk and allows lenders to extend credit under terms that conventional underwriting wouldn't otherwise support.

That guarantee changes the structural math in a few specific ways:

- **Longer amortization periods**, reducing monthly payment pressure on businesses that need time to grow into their debt
- **Lower equity requirements**, allowing borrowers with less capital to access financing for real estate, equipment, or business acquisition

- **Broader collateral flexibility**, reducing the reliance on hard collateral that young or asset-light businesses may not have
- **Access for businesses that lack conventional history**, startups, early-stage businesses, and acquisitions where the track record is limited

None of those things change the fundamentals of credit. A business still needs to demonstrate the ability to repay. Cash flow still matters. Structure still matters. What SBA changes is the *envelope*, the range of deals that can be structured soundly.

The Two Programs You Need to Understand

Most SBA lending at the front end of commercial deals involves two programs: the 7(a) and the 504. They solve different problems and are not interchangeable.

SBA 7(a): The Flexible Tool

The 7(a) is the most commonly used SBA program. It's a single loan from a single lender, partially guaranteed by the SBA, that can be used for a wide range of purposes: real estate, equipment, working capital, business acquisition, refinancing, or combinations of all of these.

Key characteristics:

- Maximum loan amount: $5 million
- Down payment: typically 10% for acquisitions and real estate; varies by purpose
- Amortization: up to 25 years for real estate, 10 years for equipment, 10 years for working capital
- Rate: variable or fixed, typically tied to Prime or SOFR plus a spread; SBA caps the maximum spread
- Guarantee: SBA guarantees 75–85% of the loan amount depending on size

The 7(a) works best when a borrower has multiple financing needs that benefit from being consolidated into a single structure, when the equity position is thin, or when conventional terms would create unsustainable payment pressure.

SBA 504: The Real Estate and Equipment Tool

The 504 is a two-loan structure designed specifically for fixed asset financing, owner-occupied real estate and long-life equipment. It splits the project into three pieces:

Source	Portion	Terms
Conventional lender (first mortgage)	50%	Bank sets terms; typically 10-year maturity, 25-year amortization
SBA debenture (second mortgage)	40%	Fixed rate, 10 or 25-year term, set at time of funding
Borrower equity	10%	Can increase to 15–20% for startups or special-use properties

The 504's fixed-rate SBA debenture is one of its strongest features for borrowers. At the time of funding, the rate is locked for the full term, which provides long-term payment certainty that variable-rate conventional financing can't match.

The 504 works best for owner-occupied real estate purchases where the borrower has sufficient equity for the 10% contribution but can't or doesn't want to put 20–25% down, and where the project cost includes renovation or buildout needs that a straight real estate loan can't cleanly accommodate.

The Front-End Question: Does SBA Solve a Structural Problem or a Credit Problem?

This is the most important distinction in SBA lending, and the one that gets confused most often.

> ***SBA should solve structural mismatches. It should never be used to justify weak fundamentals.***

A **structural mismatch** exists when a creditworthy borrower has a genuine financing need that conventional lending can't accommodate cleanly. The business is sound. The repayment story is real. But something about the conventional structure, the equity requirement, the amortization, the collateral position, creates a mismatch between what the loan needs to look like and what the business can carry.

A **credit problem** exists when the business itself isn't ready, when cash flow is too thin, history too short, or risk too high for any structure to work responsibly. SBA doesn't fix that. It just makes the mistake more official.

The test is simple: if you removed the SBA guarantee and structured this conventionally with a larger down payment or shorter amortization, would the business still be able to repay? If yes, SBA is solving a structural mismatch. If no, SBA is being asked to carry a credit decision that hasn't been made yet.

The Five Structural Mismatches SBA Solves Well

1. Equity Gap on Real Estate or Acquisitions

A business owner wants to buy their building or acquire a competitor. The deal is sound, cash flow covers debt service, the business has history, the purpose is clear. But they can't put 20–25% down without depleting operating reserves to a dangerous level.

SBA solves this by reducing the required equity contribution to 10%, preserving the borrower's working capital position. The deal that looks marginal on a conventional down payment often looks healthy on an SBA structure.

2. Amortization Mismatch on Growth-Stage Businesses

A business is profitable and growing, but conventional 10-year amortization on a term loan creates a monthly payment that strains cash flow, not because the business can't ultimately repay, but because the timing is compressed.

SBA 7(a) amortization of up to 25 years on real estate and 10 years on equipment gives the business time to grow into the debt without creating a cash flow emergency in the near term. The loan costs more in total interest. But the business survives the early years, which is the point.

3. Multipurpose Financing Needs

A borrower needs to finance a real estate purchase, fund a renovation, and have working capital for the transition, all at once. Conventional lending handles each of those separately, often requiring multiple loans with conflicting terms, overlapping collateral claims, and complicated closings.

A 7(a) can consolidate all three needs into a single structure with a single closing. That simplification isn't just convenient, it's structurally cleaner. One loan, one repayment source, one set of terms.

4. Business Acquisition with Limited Hard Collateral

Business acquisitions are one of the most common SBA use cases, and one of the most structurally challenging under conventional lending. The "collateral" in an acquisition is largely goodwill, customer relationships, and revenue, intangible assets that conventional underwriting struggles to value and secure against.

SBA's guarantee structure allows lenders to extend acquisition financing where the collateral position wouldn't otherwise support the loan. The business being acquired becomes the primary repayment source. The guarantee backstops the lender's exposure to the intangible collateral gap.

5. Startup or Early-Stage Financing

New businesses have no operating history. Conventional lending can't underwrite what doesn't exist yet. SBA's guarantee allows lenders to extend credit based on projections, owner experience, industry comparables, and equity injection, tools that conventional underwriting doesn't use because it doesn't have to.

Startup SBA deals require the most rigorous front-end work precisely because the repayment story hasn't been proven yet. The projections need to be realistic. The owner's experience needs to be relevant. The equity needs to be genuine. Getting those things right at the front end is what separates startup SBA deals that perform from ones that become problems early.

When SBA Is the Wrong Answer

Not every tight conventional deal should be an SBA deal. There are situations where reaching for SBA creates more problems than it solves.

When the business can't demonstrate repayment

If a business can't show the ability to cover debt service from operating cash flow, under normal conditions, not best-case projections, SBA doesn't change that. Longer amortization reduces the monthly payment, but it doesn't improve the underlying cash flow. If a business needs a 25-year amortization to make a loan that would normally amortize in 10 years "work," the loan probably doesn't work.

When the purpose is to refinance a structural cash flow problem

A business that has been chronically short on cash flow, running a permanently drawn line of credit, and is now looking to "clean things up" with an SBA refinance is not a structural mismatch, it's a deferred reckoning. SBA refinancing can be appropriate when it genuinely improves alignment and reduces fragility. It is not appropriate when it just extends the timeline on a problem that hasn't been solved.

When the owner is the only thing keeping the business alive

If a business depends entirely on one person, their relationships, their technical skills, their presence, and that person is also the personal guarantor, the guarantee doesn't provide the protection it appears to. SBA deals with high key-person risk need to be identified clearly at the front end, because they often look like structural mismatches when they're actually concentration risk in human form.

When SBA is being used to avoid a difficult conversation

Sometimes SBA comes up because a banker doesn't want to tell a borrower that their deal isn't ready. The longer amortization, the lower down payment, the broader eligibility criteria, it all makes a marginal deal feel possible. That's the most dangerous use of SBA at the front end, because it delays a "not yet" conversation that would have been far more helpful to the borrower than a loan that struggles from day one.

> ***SBA used to avoid a hard conversation is not a structural tool. It's a postponement.***

SBA Discovery: What to Ask at the Front End

Front-end discovery on an SBA deal follows the same logic as any commercial deal, but with a few additional questions that are specific to the structural context.

For real estate and equipment deals (504 or 7a):

- What is the total project cost, including renovation, equipment, and soft costs? (The number borrowers give first is almost always incomplete.)
- What equity is genuinely available without depleting operating reserves? (Distinguish between savings earmarked for the business and savings the borrower actually needs.)
- Does the business occupy 51% or more of the space? (Required for owner-occupied CRE eligibility.)

- What does a slow month look like after full debt service? (SBA's longer amortization is only helpful if the payment is actually manageable in the worst realistic month, not just the average.)

For acquisition deals:

- Why is the seller selling? (The honest answer to this question tells you more about the business than the financials.)
- What is the buyer's relevant experience? (The SBA guarantee doesn't make an inexperienced buyer more likely to succeed.)
- What does the transition plan look like? (Acquisitions fail most often in the first 12 months. How the buyer plans for that period is the most important front-end question.)
- Is there seller financing? (Seller participation, even a small amount held as a standby note, signals confidence and improves structure.)

For startup deals:

- Are the projections based on comparable operating businesses or built from assumptions? (One is evidence; the other is hope.)
- What is the owner's personal financial runway? (If the business is slow to ramp, how long can the owner sustain themselves without drawing from the business?)
- What has the owner done to de-risk the revenue assumptions? (Signed leases, letters of intent, presales, prior relationships, anything that moves projections toward evidence.)

> ***The right SBA discovery question is the same as every other front-end question: what would I wish I had asked if this deal becomes a problem?***

How to Talk About SBA With Borrowers

Many borrowers have heard of SBA but don't fully understand it. Some are enthusiastic because they've heard it's "easier to get." Some are resistant because they've heard the paperwork is burdensome or the process is slow. Both reactions are based on incomplete information.

The most useful front-end frame is straightforward:

> ***SBA is a tool that allows us to structure this loan in a way that fits the business. It's not a different kind of approval, it's a different kind of structure.***

When borrowers push back on SBA, it's usually about one of three things:

"The paperwork is a lot."

It is. SBA documentation requirements are more extensive than conventional lending. The honest response is to acknowledge that directly and explain what it's in exchange for: terms that wouldn't be available otherwise. If the structure genuinely fits the borrower's need, most borrowers accept the additional documentation as a reasonable trade.

"It takes too long."

SBA timelines vary significantly depending on the lender, the program, and the complexity of the deal. Preferred Lender Program (PLP) lenders can approve 7(a) loans in-house without SBA review, which dramatically reduces turnaround time. If timeline is a genuine concern, the right conversation is about lender selection and process management, not about avoiding SBA.

"I don't want the government involved in my business."

This is more emotional than practical. The SBA guarantee is a lender-facing mechanism, it doesn't give the government any operational oversight of the business. The reporting requirements on SBA loans are no more intrusive than standard commercial loan covenants. The honest response is to clarify what SBA involvement actually means and doesn't mean.

SBA and the Warning Signs

All ten warning signs from Chapter 10 apply to SBA deals. But a few deserve particular attention in the SBA context because they're easier to miss when the structure feels more accommodating.

Repayment that depends on "next year"

SBA's longer amortization can make a deal feel workable even when the underlying cash flow story is too thin. A business projecting 40% revenue growth in year two to support debt service is not a structural mismatch, it's an optimism problem with a longer runway. The front-end question is the same: does the loan work *before* improvement, not because of it?

Guarantees doing all the work

SBA requires personal guarantees from all owners with 20% or more ownership. That's appropriate. But when the primary argument for an SBA deal is the strength of the guarantor's personal financial statement, rather than the business's ability to repay, the structure is off. The guarantee should reinforce a sound deal, not rescue a fragile one.

One loan trying to fix everything

The flexibility of the SBA 7(a), its ability to consolidate multiple needs into a single loan, is one of its genuine strengths. It's also one of its most common misuses. A 7(a) that's trying to buy real estate, fund renovation, pay off an existing line, provide working capital, and finance equipment all at once is usually doing too much. The consolidation should simplify the structure. If it's just bundling complexity, it's not a solution, it's a deferral.

7(a) vs. 504: A Quick Decision Framework

If the deal looks like…	Consider 7(a)	Consider 504
Single-purpose real estate purchase	If borrower needs one loan and full flexibility	Preferred, fixed rate on SBA portion, lower monthly cost
Real estate + renovation	If construction component is complex or phased	Works well if renovation is included in project cost at closing
Business acquisition	Primary tool, 7(a) handles goodwill and intangibles	Not designed for acquisitions
Equipment only	Yes, 7(a) up to 10-year amortization	504 works for large, long-life equipment
Multipurpose (RE + equipment + working capital)	Yes, consolidation is 7(a)'s strength	Not designed for mixed purposes
Startup financing	Yes, if projections are realistic and equity is genuine	Possible but less common

This framework is a starting point, not a rule. Every deal has specifics that matter. The right program is always the one that produces a structure the business can actually carry.

A Final Front-End Principle

SBA lending can feel like it operates by different rules than conventional commercial lending. In some procedural ways, it does. But at the front end, where structure is shaped and outcomes are determined, the same principles apply without exception.

The five front-end questions still govern every SBA deal:

1. What is really happening inside this business?
2. Why does this business need debt right now?
3. How will this loan be repaid under normal conditions?
4. What happens if things don't go as planned?
5. Does the structure fit the risk?

SBA expands the range of structures available for answering those questions. It doesn't change what the questions are.

> ***A banker who understands SBA as a structuring tool, not a product or a shortcut, will build better deals, have better credit conversations, and serve borrowers more honestly than one who reaches for it out of habit or avoidance.***

That's the standard. Hold it on every SBA deal you touch.

CHAPTER 7

Pricing, Rate, and the Value You Actually Provide

Of all the conversations in commercial lending, the rate conversation is the one that makes newer bankers most uncomfortable.

Not because it's technically complex. It isn't. The discomfort comes from something else: most bankers haven't been given a framework for thinking about pricing that's any more sophisticated than "this is what the system generated." So when a borrower pushes back on rate, and they will, the banker either defends a number they don't fully understand or backs down from it in a way that signals the rate wasn't well-reasoned to begin with.

This chapter is not about rate-setting mechanics. Your institution has processes for that, and they exist for good reasons. This chapter is about how to *think* about pricing, how rate connects to risk and structure, how to explain it without apologizing for it, and how to understand whether a deal is actually profitable in the way that matters for your institution and your borrowers over time.

> ***Rate is not the primary way a banker creates value. Structure is. A banker who understands that can have a completely different pricing conversation than one who doesn't.***

What Rate Is Actually Doing

Interest rate has one fundamental job: to compensate the bank for the risk and cost of extending credit over time. That's it.

When a bank lends money, it takes on several things simultaneously: the risk that the borrower can't repay, the cost of the capital being deployed, the administrative cost of managing the relationship, and the opportunity cost of not deploying that capital elsewhere. Rate is the mechanism by which the bank is compensated for all of those things.

This means rate is not arbitrary. It's not a negotiating position. It's a signal, and the signal it sends is worth understanding.

Higher rate signals

- More uncertainty in the repayment story
- Longer exposure to changing conditions
- Less structural protection, weaker collateral, thinner cash flow, less history
- More complexity in monitoring and management over the life of the loan

Lower rate signals

- Strong, predictable cash flow
- Well-collateralized position
- Short exposure window
- Simple, clean structure with limited monitoring needs

When a borrower asks why their rate is what it is, a banker who understands these signals can give an honest, specific answer. Not "that's what the system generated," not "that's our standard rate for this product," but: "here's what the structure looks like and here's what the rate is compensating for." That's a different conversation, and a more credible one.

Rate and Structure Are Connected

This is the insight that changes how bankers think about pricing, and it's almost never taught explicitly.

> ***Rate and structure are not separate conversations. They are the same conversation viewed from different angles. When structure improves, rate often follows. When structure is weak, rate carries more of the risk, and can only carry so much of it.***

Think about what happens when a borrower comes in with a weak collateral position. The bank can respond in one of three ways: decline the deal, accept the weak collateral and price for the risk, or improve the structure, perhaps by adding a personal guarantee, shortening the term, or right-sizing the amount, and price accordingly.

The third option is almost always the most useful. It creates a deal that works for the borrower, works for the bank, and prices appropriately for the actual risk rather than the default risk. The banker who thinks this way isn't competing on rate. They're competing on structure, which is a much more durable competitive advantage.

Practically, this means that before having any pricing conversation with a borrower, the structure should already be set. Rate should follow structure, not precede it. A banker who quotes a rate before the structure is finalized is quoting a number without a foundation.

The rate-structure tradeoff in practice

Consider two versions of the same deal: a $350,000 equipment loan for a seven-year-old manufacturer.

Element	Version A	Version B
Amortization	10 years	7 years
Collateral	Equipment only	Equipment + A/R lien
Guarantee	Personal guarantee	Personal guarantee
Risk profile	Higher, longer exposure, thinner collateral	Lower, faster burn-down, added collateral layer
Appropriate rate	Higher	Lower

Version B is not just cheaper for the borrower. It's better structured. The rate difference reflects the risk difference. When the banker explains it this way, the borrower isn't being asked to accept a lower rate as a gift, they're being shown how to earn it through better structure. That's a fundamentally different conversation than "I got you a better rate."

The Rate Conversation With Borrowers

Borrowers focus on rate more than almost any other element of a loan. This is understandable, rate is the number that's easiest to compare across lenders, easiest to put in a spreadsheet, and easiest to use as a proxy for whether they're getting a good deal.

The problem is that rate is often not the most important variable. A loan at a lower rate with the wrong structure, wrong term, wrong amortization, wrong product, costs a borrower far more in stress, inflexibility, and eventual restructuring than a loan at a slightly higher rate with structure that actually fits.

> ***The most expensive loan a borrower can take is one that doesn't fit their business, regardless of the rate on it.***

When a borrower pushes back on rate

Rate pushback is one of the most common front-end conversations, and most bankers handle it badly, either by apologizing for the rate, which signals it might be negotiable, or by defending it with technical language the borrower doesn't follow, which signals the banker doesn't really understand it either.

The better approach has three moves:

- Acknowledge the question directly: "Rate is always worth understanding. Let me explain what's driving it."
- Connect it to structure and risk: "The rate reflects the term we're using and the collateral position we're working with. Here's what each of those means for this deal."

- Offer the structural lever if it exists: "If we shortened the term or added a lien on the receivables, the rate would come down. Here's what that would do to your payment. Is that worth exploring?"

That third move is important. It shifts the conversation from "will you lower the rate?" to "do you want to change the structure?" Those are very different questions. The first is a negotiation. The second is a structural conversation, which is exactly the conversation a banker should be having.

A short version of this in practice:

> **Borrower:** "I was quoted 7.5% at another bank. Can you match it?"
>
> **Banker:** "I want to make sure we're comparing the same thing before I answer that. What was the term and amortization on their quote?"
>
> **Borrower:** "I'm not sure. Ten years, I think."
>
> **Banker:** "Okay. Our quote is on a seven-year amortization, which is why the rate looks different, shorter exposure, faster principal paydown. If we matched the ten-year term their rate makes more sense, but your total interest cost over the life of the loan actually goes up even though the rate looks better. Want me to show you the two side by side?"

> **Note:** The banker doesn't defend the rate or compete on it. They reframe the comparison so the borrower is evaluating total cost and structural fit rather than rate in isolation. That's the conversation a confident, well-informed banker has.

Transaction Pricing vs. Relationship Pricing

Not every deal should be priced the same way. A single transaction with a borrower you've never met is priced differently from the entry point into a relationship with a growing business you expect to deepen over years. Understanding the difference, and being intentional about which one you're doing, is part of thinking about pricing at a professional level.

Transaction pricing

Transaction pricing starts with the deal itself. What is the risk? What is the appropriate compensation for that risk? What does the market support for this type and term of credit? The price is set to make the individual deal work for the bank on a standalone basis.

This is the right framework for a borrower you don't know well, a one-time financing need, or a deal where the relationship has no clear expansion path.

Relationship pricing

Relationship pricing considers the full picture: the deposit relationship, the operating accounts, the ancillary services, the potential for future deals, the referral value, the long-term revenue stream. A deal priced slightly tighter than standalone analysis would justify can make sense if the relationship economics support it, if the bank is capturing enough of the total relationship to make the full picture work.

The critical discipline in relationship pricing is that it has to be conscious and documented. "I priced it a little tighter because I like this borrower" is not relationship pricing. It's imprecision. The banker who can say "I priced this 25 basis points inside our standard because the full deposit and operating relationship generates X in annual fee income and this loan is the anchor to that relationship" is making a defensible professional judgment.

The mistake to avoid

The most common pricing mistake in commercial lending isn't pricing too high. It's pricing too low without knowing why, competing on rate because structure felt too complicated to explain, or backing down from a well-reasoned price because the borrower pushed back.

> ***A banker who competes primarily on rate is telling the market they have nothing else to offer. Structure, guidance, flexibility, and long-term partnership are more durable competitive***

> ***advantages than basis points, but only if the banker can articulate them.***

Understanding Relationship Profitability

This book has focused almost entirely on individual deals. But banks, and bankers, think about relationships. A deal that looks strong in isolation might be part of a relationship that isn't generating adequate return. A deal that looks tight on rate might be anchored to a relationship that's highly profitable overall.

Newer commercial bankers don't need to run full relationship profitability models. But they do need to understand the concept well enough to have honest conversations about it, with credit, with senior lenders, and eventually with borrowers.

What goes into relationship profitability

A commercial banking relationship generates revenue from multiple sources: loan interest, fee income on the loan itself, deposit balances and the net interest income they generate, treasury and cash management services, and in some cases referral fees or other ancillary revenue. The relationship is profitable when the total revenue from all of those sources exceeds the cost of managing the relationship and the risk-adjusted cost of the capital deployed.

The practical implication for front-end bankers is this: a deal that looks marginal on rate might be worth doing if it anchors a full operating relationship. A deal that looks strong on rate might be worth pricing more carefully if it's one piece of a shallow relationship that will never generate the ancillary revenue that justifies the credit exposure.

The deposit conversation

One of the most underleveraged conversations in commercial lending is the deposit conversation. A borrower who moves their operating accounts to the lending bank creates a relationship that generates value beyond the loan, and those balances provide the bank with a clearer picture of the business's actual cash flow than any financial statement can.

The banker who makes the deposit conversation a natural part of the deal conversation, not as a condition of the loan, but as a genuine recommendation, is building relationships that perform better on every dimension: credit quality, profitability, and early warning on potential problems.

What Bankers Can't Control, and What They Can

Newer bankers sometimes feel frustrated by pricing because so much of it is set by processes outside their control, rate floors, spread guidelines, risk-based pricing models. That frustration is understandable but often misdirected.

What a banker can't control: the base rate environment, the institution's cost of funds, the credit risk rating assigned to a borrower, the rate floor for a given product or risk tier.

What a banker **can** control: the structure that determines the risk rating, the amortization that affects the rate tier, the collateral position that influences the pricing, the completeness of the relationship that affects how the deal is viewed overall. In other words, the banker can't set the rate directly, but they have significant influence over the inputs that drive it.

> ***The banker who understands the pricing inputs builds better structures. The banker who just accepts the output builds deals by accident.***

A Simple Pricing Discipline

Before any rate conversation with a borrower, ask yourself three questions:

- Does this rate reflect the actual risk in this structure, and can I explain why?
- Have I competed on structure first, so that rate is a reflection of the deal rather than a starting point for negotiation?
- Am I pricing a transaction or a relationship, and have I made that choice consciously?

A banker who can answer those three questions confidently will never be caught defending a number they don't understand. They will also never lose a deal on rate that they should have won on structure.

> ***The banker who competes on structure doesn't need to compete on rate. That's not an accident. It's the point.***

In the next chapter, we'll build on this structural thinking by developing pattern recognition across specific business types, how cash flows differently in different industries, and how those differences shape the loans that work best for each one.

CHAPTER 8

General Terms, Explained

For many bankers, general terms are where confidence starts to wobble.

The words sound formal. The implications feel heavy. And too often, they're treated like technical details best left to credit, something to deal with later, after the borrower is already committed.

That's a mistake.

General terms are not fine print. They are **signals**. They tell you what the bank is worried about, how risk is being managed, and where a deal might still be fragile. Bankers who understand them can prepare borrowers better, adjust structure earlier, and arrive at credit with far fewer surprises.

General Terms Are Not Punishments

Let's start by clearing something up.

General terms are not a lack of trust, a judgment on character, or a sign that credit doesn't like the deal. They are simply how banks translate uncertainty into discipline.

Every commercial loan assumes something will change. Revenue fluctuates. Costs rise. Customers behave unpredictably. Owners get distracted. General terms exist to make sure the bank notices *early*, not after damage is done.

> ***Seen correctly, general terms protect both sides of the relationship.***

The Five Categories of General Terms

Most general terms fall into five broad categories. You don't need to memorize legal language. You need to understand the intent behind each one.

- Pricing and rate structure

- Maturity and renewal
- Financial expectations
- Reporting and information flow
- Limitations on behavior

Each category tells a story about where the bank sees risk, and how it's being managed.

Interest Rate: Pricing Risk, Not People

Interest rates get more attention than they deserve at the front end. From a structural perspective, rates exist to compensate for risk, reflect the nature of the loan, and encourage appropriate use of credit.

Rates are influenced by loan type, term length, predictability of cash flow, and the overall strength of structure. They are not moral judgments. A higher rate usually signals more uncertainty, longer exposure, or less flexibility in structure.

When borrowers focus only on rate, they miss the bigger picture:

> ***A slightly higher rate on a well-structured loan is almost always cheaper than a low rate on a bad one.***

Maturity and Renewal: Forced Conversations

Maturity dates are not just calendar items. They exist to create intentional moments of review.

Shorter maturities force regular reassessment, limit long-term exposure, and encourage ongoing engagement. Longer maturities reduce friction and increase comfort, but they also assume stability that may not hold.

For lines of credit, maturity often matters more than amortization. A one-year line with annual review is the bank saying: "We expect this to revolve, and we want to check in regularly." That's discipline, not distrust.

Financial Expectations: Early Warning, Not Enforcement

Financial terms, often called covenants, make many bankers nervous. They shouldn't.

At their core, covenants exist to establish expectations, identify trends, and trigger conversations before problems grow. They are not designed to create defaults. They are designed to prevent surprises.

The most important front-end question isn't whether the covenants are tight. It's whether they match how the business actually operates. Good terms align with reality. Bad ones ignore it.

When covenants are breached, the issue is rarely the math. It's usually a mismatch between the structure and how the business actually runs, which means the real fix happens at the front end, not in the workout.

Reporting Requirements: Staying Visible

Banks don't ask for information because they're curious. They ask because distance creates risk.

Reporting terms keep the relationship current, reduce guesswork, and surface problems early. More reporting generally signals complexity, volatility, or significant change. Less reporting signals stability, predictability, and simplicity.

At the front end, your role is to anticipate what information credit will need, how often the business can realistically provide it, and whether those expectations are reasonable. Good reporting requirements feel routine, not burdensome.

Limitations on Behavior: Guardrails, Not Handcuffs

Some general terms restrict what a borrower can do: take on additional debt, sell assets, make large owner distributions, or make major changes to the business.

These exist for one reason: to keep the risk profile from changing without a conversation. Banks are comfortable with risk they understand. They are uncomfortable with surprises.

A borrower who understands this usually has no issue with reasonable limits, because they're already thinking long-term. Resistance usually signals a misunderstanding, not hostility.

How to Talk About General Terms at the Front End

This is where bankers add real value, not by explaining terms defensively or apologizing for them, but by framing them as tools for a healthy relationship.

The language matters. Instead of "credit requires this," try "this helps us manage risk early." Instead of "we need protection," try "this gives us room if things change." Instead of "these are covenants," try "these are check-in points."

When general terms are explained calmly and connected to the borrower's own goals, most borrowers accept them easily. Resistance almost always means misunderstanding, not hostility.

What General Terms Reveal About a Deal

If you read general terms carefully, they tell a story.

They reveal where credit sees risk, what structural element is carrying the most weight, how confident the bank is in the borrower's stability, and where flexibility exists, and where it doesn't.

That's useful information, not just for understanding the deal, but for improving it. Bankers who read terms this way can prepare borrowers better, adjust structure earlier, and reduce friction at every stage.

A Common Front-End Mistake

One of the most common mistakes is treating general terms as something to negotiate *after* approval. That's backwards.

General terms reflect structure. If they feel uncomfortable, to you or to the borrower, the structure may still be off. When terms feel punitive, it's often because the loan is doing too much work, or the wrong work.

> ***Fix structure first. Terms usually soften on their own.***

A Simple Test

Before moving a deal forward, ask yourself:

"If I were the borrower, would these terms make sense given how the business actually runs?"

If the answer is no, don't argue with credit. Go back to structure.

Understanding general terms doesn't require legal training. It requires empathy, clarity, and discipline. When you understand *why* terms exist, they stop being intimidating, and start becoming useful.

In the next chapter, we'll walk through the front-end process flow: how commercial loans actually move from conversation to structure to credit, and where bankers make the biggest difference along the way.

PART III
LOAN TYPES

What you must know before you submit any of these four instruments.

These four chapters belong at the front of your preparation for any commercial deal. Each one follows the same structure: what the instrument is, when it's the right tool, what you must know before you submit, what credit will look for, where these deals die, and the discovery questions you need to ask before the file is half-built.

Read the chapter for any loan type before you submit one. Not after the borrower has committed. Not after you've collected the financials. Before.

The banker who walks into a construction loan discovery call without understanding draw mechanics, inspections, and interest reserves is collecting information they don't yet know how to use. These chapters are designed to fix that.

CHAPTER 9

SBA Loans: What You Need to Know Before You Submit

The most misused structuring tool in commercial lending, and the most powerful one when applied correctly.

What This Instrument Actually Is

The SBA does not lend money. It guarantees a portion of loans made by approved lenders, which reduces the bank's risk and allows the lender to extend credit under terms that conventional underwriting wouldn't otherwise support. That guarantee, typically 75 to 85 percent of the loan amount, is what changes the structural math.

The two programs a front-end banker needs to understand are the 7(a) and the 504. They are not interchangeable. The 7(a) is a single loan from a single lender that can fund almost any business purpose, real estate, equipment, acquisition, working capital, or combinations. The 504 is a two-loan structure designed specifically for fixed asset financing: owner-occupied real estate and long-life equipment, split between a conventional first mortgage and a fixed-rate SBA debenture.

Everything else about SBA, the paperwork, the timeline, the eligibility rules, is process. The instrument itself is a structural tool that solves a specific problem: the gap between what a sound business needs and what conventional lending can comfortably provide.

When It's the Right Tool

SBA is the right tool when a creditworthy borrower has a genuine financing need that conventional lending can't accommodate cleanly, not because the business is weak, but because the structure doesn't fit. Five conditions make SBA appropriate:

Equity gap.

The borrower can't put 20 to 25 percent down without depleting operating reserves to a dangerous level. SBA reduces the required equity contribution to 10 percent, preserving working capital. The deal that looks marginal on a conventional down payment often looks healthy on an SBA structure.

Amortization mismatch.

Conventional 10-year amortization creates a monthly payment that strains cash flow, not because the business can't ultimately repay, but because the timing is compressed. SBA's longer amortization gives the business time to grow into the debt.

Multipurpose financing needs.

The borrower needs to finance a real estate purchase, fund a renovation, and have working capital for the transition, all at once. A 7(a) can consolidate those needs into a single structure with a single closing.

Business acquisition with limited hard collateral.

The asset being acquired is largely goodwill, customer relationships, and revenue, intangibles that conventional underwriting struggles to secure against. SBA's guarantee allows the lender to extend acquisition financing where the collateral position wouldn't otherwise support the loan.

Startup or early-stage financing.

The business has no operating history. SBA allows lenders to extend credit based on projections, owner experience, and equity injection, tools conventional underwriting doesn't use because it doesn't have to.

SBA is the wrong tool when the business can't demonstrate repayment from operating cash flow, when it's being used to refinance a structural problem that hasn't been solved, or when it's being reached for because a banker doesn't want to tell a borrower their deal isn't ready.

> ***SBA used to avoid a difficult conversation is not a structural tool. It's a postponement.***

What You Must Know Before You Submit

7(a) key terms:

- Maximum loan amount: $5 million
- Down payment: typically 10% for acquisitions and real estate; varies by purpose
- Amortization: up to 25 years for real estate, 10 years for equipment, 10 years for working capital
- Rate: variable or fixed, tied to Prime or SOFR plus a spread; SBA caps the maximum spread
- Guarantee: SBA guarantees 75–85% depending on loan size
- Personal guarantee required from all owners with 20% or more ownership

504 structure:

Source	Terms
Conventional lender (first mortgage) 50%	Bank sets terms; typically 10-year maturity, 25-year amortization
SBA debenture (second mortgage) 40%	Fixed rate, 10 or 25-year term, locked at time of funding
Borrower equity 10%	Increases to 15–20% for startups or special-use properties

Eligibility rules to verify before going further:

- Business must be for-profit and operate in the United States
- Owner-occupied CRE requires the borrower to occupy at least 51% of the space

- Certain industries are ineligible, financial businesses, lending institutions, passive real estate investment, verify with your SBA department
- All owners with 20% or more must provide personal guarantees and personal financial statements
- The business must have been unable to obtain conventional financing on reasonable terms

Preferred Lender Program (PLP):

Lenders with PLP status can approve 7(a) loans in-house without SBA review. This dramatically reduces turnaround time. Know whether your institution is a PLP lender and what that means for timeline expectations with borrowers.

What credit will look for:

✓ Repayment from operations, not projections, debt service coverage must work under normal conditions, slow months included

✓ Equity injection verification, genuine equity from the borrower's own resources, not a borrowed source

✓ Use of proceeds completeness, total project cost fully accounted for, including soft costs and renovation contingencies

✓ Transition plan for acquisitions, credible answer to what happens in the first 90 days for customers, staff, and suppliers

✓ Personal financial strength of guarantors, resources to support the business through adversity if needed

Where these deals die:

⚠ Total project cost underestimated, borrower discovers mid-process they need more than the loan covers

⚠ Equity injection not verified as genuinely available without depleting operating reserves

⚠ Eligibility not confirmed before significant time is invested, the business or purpose is ineligible

⚠ Wrong SBA program chosen, 504 presented for an acquisition, 7(a) for a deal where 504 would be cleaner

⚠ DSCR works on average but breaks on a slow month, coverage built on best-case, not normal-case

⚠ Acquisition transition plan is vague, "the seller will be available to help" is not a transition plan

⚠ Borrower has outstanding tax liabilities not disclosed, SBA requires these to be resolved at closing

Discovery questions, ask before the file is half-built:

→ What is the total project cost, including renovation, equipment, soft costs, and working capital needs? (The first number a borrower gives is almost always incomplete.)

→ What equity is genuinely available without depleting operating reserves?

→ What does a slow month look like after full debt service? (The payment has to work in January, not just in July.)

→ Are there any outstanding tax liabilities, judgments, or existing SBA loans?

→ Does the business occupy, or will it occupy, at least 51% of the space? (For real estate deals.)

→ Why is the seller selling? (For acquisitions, the honest answer tells you more than the financials.)

→ What is the buyer's relevant experience in this industry or business type?

→ Is there any seller financing, even a small seller note signals confidence and improves structure.

→ Are the revenue projections based on comparable operating businesses, or built from assumptions? (For startups.)

→ What is the owner's personal financial runway if the business is slow to ramp?

CHAPTER 10

Construction Loans: What You Need to Know Before You Submit

The most complex instrument in commercial lending, and the one where front-end preparation matters most.

What This Instrument Actually Is

A construction loan is a short-term credit facility that funds the cost of building or substantially renovating a property, disbursed in stages as work is completed, rather than in a single advance at closing. It is not a permanent loan. It is bridge financing that connects the start of construction to the completion of a project that will then be refinanced into permanent financing.

The mechanics are fundamentally different from any other loan type. The collateral doesn't fully exist at origination. The loan balance grows over time as draws are made rather than declining as payments are made. The repayment source during construction is typically interest-only, often funded from an interest reserve built into the loan, with principal repayment deferred until the permanent loan closes at project completion.

> ***Three things define construction lending: disbursement in stages, collateral that's being built, and interest-only with a reserve. Understand these before your first conversation.***

When It's the Right Tool

New construction.

A borrower is building a facility from the ground up, owner-occupied commercial real estate, an investment property, or a residential development.

Substantial renovation.

An existing property is being renovated to the point where it can't be occupied during construction, or where the renovation cost is significant enough relative to property value that it resembles a new construction project in risk profile.

Construction-to-permanent.

The same lender provides both the construction loan and the permanent financing, with a single closing and automatic conversion at project completion. This is the cleanest structure for owner-occupied CRE.

Stand-alone construction with a takeout commitment.

The construction lender is not providing the permanent financing. The borrower has a commitment from another lender, or expects to arrange permanent financing at completion. This structure carries more risk because the takeout is not guaranteed.

What You Must Know Before You Submit

The draw process, know this before you speak to the borrower:

Construction loans disburse in draws, periodic advances against the loan balance as work is completed. Before each draw is funded, the lender typically requires:

- A draw request from the borrower or contractor documenting work completed and costs incurred
- An inspection by a third-party inspector confirming the work is complete and the cost is reasonable
- Lien waivers from contractors and subcontractors for work funded in prior draws
- A title update confirming no mechanic's liens have been filed since the last draw

The draw process is not a formality. Lenders who fund draws without inspection and lien waivers create exposure to mechanic's liens, cost overruns, and fraud. Understand it because borrowers will ask about it.

The interest reserve:

During construction, the borrower isn't generating income from the property and often doesn't want to make cash interest payments out of pocket. An interest reserve is an amount built into the loan at origination to fund the interest payments during the construction period. It must be sized correctly for the loan amount, the interest rate, the construction timeline, and the expected draw schedule. An interest reserve that's too small runs out before the project completes, leaving the borrower with unexpected cash payments or a loan in technical default. Calculate it conservatively with a buffer for schedule delays.

The contingency reserve:

Construction projects run over budget. A standard contingency is 5 to 10 percent of hard construction costs for established contractors on standard projects; higher for complex projects, new construction types, or less experienced contractors. If it's not there and costs overrun, the borrower funds the difference from cash, which may or may not exist.

Hard costs vs. soft costs:

Hard costs are direct construction costs, labor, materials, contractor fees. Soft costs are indirect project costs, architectural and engineering fees, permits and approvals, legal fees, lender fees, insurance during construction, and the interest reserve itself. Soft costs often run 15 to 25 percent of total project cost. A budget that only accounts for hard costs is incomplete.

Fixed-price contract vs. estimate:

A fixed-price contract commits the general contractor to complete the project for a defined price. Cost overruns become the contractor's problem. An estimate or cost-plus contract means overruns flow through to the borrower. This is a material difference in risk profile. Always know which one you're working with.

LTV on construction loans:

Construction loan LTV is based on the "as-completed" appraised value, what the property will be worth when the project is finished, not what it's worth today. This means the appraisal is a projection, not a fact. Projects that come in over budget, on delayed timelines, or into a changed market can produce a completed property worth less than the appraisal assumed.

What credit will look for:

✓ Contractor qualification, licensed, bonded, insured, with comparable completed projects as evidence

✓ Project budget completeness, hard costs, soft costs, interest reserve, and contingency all accounted for

✓ Takeout qualification, credible permanent financing plan with prequalification evidence for nonconversion structures

✓ Borrower equity, typically 20–25% of total project cost contributed before first draw

✓ Appraisal assumptions, comparable sales and income assumptions reviewed for reasonableness in current market conditions

Where these deals die:

⚠️ Budget is incomplete, soft costs and interest reserve are missing, creating a funding gap that surfaces mid-construction

⚠️ Contractor is unqualified or unverified, license, bond, and insurance not confirmed before the file is built

⚠️ No fixed-price contract, cost overrun risk hasn't been addressed in the contingency budget

⚠️ Draws funded without completed inspections, exposure to work that wasn't done and costs that weren't incurred

⚠︎ Lien waivers not collected, mechanic's liens can cloud title and impair the lender's security position

⚠︎ Interest reserve runs out before project completes, borrower isn't prepared to fund interest from cash

⚠︎ Project completes but borrower can't qualify for permanent financing, construction lender left holding a completed property with no exit

Discovery questions, ask before the file is half-built:

→ What is the total project cost, hard costs, soft costs, permits, architect, and financing costs combined?

→ Is there a fixed-price contract in place, or is this a cost-plus or estimate arrangement?

→ What contingency has been budgeted for cost overruns?

→ Has the contractor completed a comparable project in the last three years? Can they provide references?

→ What is the expected construction timeline from groundbreaking to certificate of occupancy?

→ What buffer is built into the timeline for weather delays, permit delays, or material lead times?

→ Will the permanent financing come from this institution, or does the borrower have a commitment elsewhere?

→ If permanent financing is external, has the borrower prequalified? What are the conditions?

→ How much equity is the borrower contributing, and when will it be injected?

→ If the project runs over budget by 10 to 15 percent, how would that be funded?

CHAPTER 11

Real Estate Loans: What You Need to Know Before You Submit

Tangible collateral creates confidence. That confidence is sometimes wrong.

What This Instrument Actually Is

A commercial real estate loan is a term loan secured by a first mortgage on commercial property, with repayment coming from the income generated by the property, the operations of the business occupying it, or both. It is a long-term instrument with a long exposure window.

The two most common types a front-end banker will encounter are owner-occupied CRE, where the borrower's business operates in the property, and investor or income-producing CRE, where the property is leased to tenants and cash flow depends on rents. These are fundamentally different credit underwriting exercises, even though both involve real estate as collateral. Conflating them is one of the most common front-end errors in commercial real estate lending.

When It's the Right Tool

Owner-occupied CRE

Appropriate when the borrower's business has stable, predictable cash flow that supports the debt service; when ownership genuinely reduces long-term occupancy cost or risk compared to leasing; and when the business is mature enough that the real estate investment won't strain operational flexibility. Buying a building should strengthen the business, not rescue it.

Investment or income-producing CRE

Appropriate when the property generates sufficient net operating income to cover debt service with a meaningful cushion; when the tenancy is stable and leases are long enough to support the loan term;

and when the borrower has the experience and resources to manage the property through tenant transitions and capital expenditures.

> ***Real estate should support the business, not rescue it.***

What You Must Know Before You Submit

The two repayment sources, and which one is actually primary:

Owner-occupied CRE has two potential repayment sources: the cash flow of the business occupying the property, and the value of the property itself. The business cash flow is primary. The real estate is collateral. A banker who underwrites an owner-occupied CRE deal primarily on real estate value has confused the collateral with the credit.

Investment CRE has one primary repayment source: the net operating income of the property. If the NOI doesn't cover the debt service, the deal isn't structured correctly regardless of appraised value.

DSCR and LTV, they measure different things:

For owner-occupied CRE, Debt Service Coverage Ratio is calculated on the business's total cash flow against all obligations. Most lenders require a minimum of 1.20x to 1.25x. For investment CRE, DSCR is calculated on the net operating income of the property, gross rental income minus vacancy allowance minus operating expenses. The vacancy allowance is not optional. A fully leased building is not a stable assumption for the life of a commercial loan.

LTV is the ratio of the loan amount to the appraised value, most conventional CRE lenders lend to 75 to 80 percent. LTV protects the lender's position if the property must be sold. It does not measure the borrower's ability to repay. Both metrics matter and both need to be understood independently.

Special-use properties, identify before you go in:

A special-use property has limited alternative uses, a car wash, a funeral home, a gas station, a bowling alley. These properties are worth significantly less as collateral because the buyer pool if the borrower defaults is narrow. Most lenders require higher equity and apply greater scrutiny. Identify special-use situations before the borrower has invested time in a conventional underwriting process.

Lease analysis for investment CRE:

Before submitting an investment CRE deal, understand the tenant profile: who are the tenants, how long are the leases, when do they expire, is there anchor tenant concentration, and what are the renewal options? A building that's 95 percent leased today with three leases expiring in 18 months is a fundamentally different credit from a building with 10-year leases across diverse tenants.

Environmental due diligence:

Always ask whether the borrower knows of any environmental issues with the property before the appraisal is ordered. For properties with prior industrial use, gas stations, dry cleaners, or other potential contamination sources, a Phase II environmental assessment may be required. Environmental issues can render a property worthless as collateral and stop a transaction entirely.

What credit will look for:

✓ Business cash flow for owner-occupied, total obligations analyzed, not just the new real estate loan

✓ Vacancy and expense assumptions for investment CRE: NOI stress-tested at realistic vacancy levels

✓ Lease terms relative to loan term, rollover risk identified and addressed for deals with short remaining lease terms

✓ Environmental status, Phase I Environmental Site Assessment for all commercial transactions

✓ Global cash flow, borrower's other properties and personal obligations modeled alongside the subject deal

Where these deals die:

⚠️ Owner-occupied deal underwritten on real estate value rather than business cash flow, DSCR problem surfaces at credit

⚠️ Special-use property not identified early, conventional LTV assumptions don't apply

⚠️ Total debt load not modeled, new real estate loan stacks on existing obligations and breaks coverage

⚠️ Environmental issue not surfaced, Phase I reveals contamination that stops the transaction

⚠️ Appraisal uses aggressive cap rate assumptions, credit orders a review or applies haircuts

⚠️ Investment CRE lease analysis reveals near-term rollover risk not disclosed in the submission

⚠️ Title search reveals existing liens or encumbrances not disclosed at application

Discovery questions, ask before the file is half-built:

→ How long has the business been at its current location, and what are the current total occupancy costs? (For owner-occupied.)

→ Does the business have any existing debt that needs to be modeled alongside the real estate loan?

→ Is this a standard commercial property or does it have limited alternative uses?

→ Is there any known environmental history at the site?

→ Who are the tenants, how long are the leases, and when do the major leases expire? (For investment CRE.)

→ What is the current vacancy rate, and what has it been over the last three years?

→ Are any tenants on month-to-month arrangements that don't show in the rent roll?

→ What are the annual capital expenditure needs, roof, HVAC, parking lot?

CHAPTER 12

C&I Loans: What You Need to Know Before You Submit

The loan type where the business itself is the collateral, and understanding the business is the only real protection.

What This Instrument Actually Is

Commercial and Industrial lending, C&I, is the broadest category in commercial lending and the one that most directly requires a banker to understand how a business actually works. C&I loans are extended to operating businesses for working capital, equipment, business acquisition, or other operational purposes, and the primary repayment source is almost always the cash flow of the business itself, not the liquidation of a hard asset.

This distinction matters. Real estate loans can fall back on the property. Equipment loans can fall back on the collateral. C&I loans fall back on the business, which means the banker's front-end understanding of the business is not just helpful. It's the underwriting.

C&I loans take several forms: revolving lines of credit, term loans for equipment or business investment, asset-based lending facilities where the line is secured by and sized to eligible receivables and inventory, and acquisition or buyout financing. Each has different mechanics, but all share the same fundamental requirement: the banker must understand how the business generates cash and whether that cash flow is durable.

When It's the Right Tool

A business has a recurring operating cycle with a cash gap.

Working capital lines exist to bridge the timing difference between when cash goes out and when it comes back in. A manufacturer who pays for raw materials today and collects from customers in 60 days needs the line to fund that gap. That's the instrument doing its job.

A business needs to invest in an asset that generates returns over time.

Equipment that increases capacity, reduces cost, or extends the business's productive life is a sound reason for a term loan. The asset should have a measurable life, and the amortization should match it.

A business is being acquired and the primary value is intangible.

Goodwill, customer relationships, workforce, and proprietary processes are C&I assets. Business acquisition financing is C&I even when real estate is part of the transaction, because the primary repayment source is the acquired business's cash flow.

A business has significant receivables and inventory that support a borrowing base.

Asset-based lending is a more sophisticated form of C&I financing suited to businesses with substantial balance sheets, manufacturers, distributors, staffing firms, where the eligible asset base justifies a line larger than cash flow analysis alone would support.

What You Must Know Before You Submit

The operating cycle, the most important concept in C&I lending:

Every business has an operating cycle: the sequence of events from when cash goes out to fund operations until cash comes back in from customers. Understanding the operating cycle is the foundation for every C&I structure. A line of credit should be sized to the cash gap in the operating cycle, not to a round number the borrower requested.

Lines vs. term loans, the most common structural error:

The most common mistake in C&I lending is using a line of credit to fund a need that should be a term loan. Lines are for temporary, recurring needs that resolve within the operating cycle. Term loans are for permanent investments with a measurable life. A business that has been fully drawn on its line for 18 months doesn't have a working capital need, it has a permanent capital need disguised as a revolving facility. That structure needs to be unwound, not renewed.

> ***A permanently drawn line is not a line. It's term debt with no discipline. Identify it early.***

Borrowing base basics:

For businesses with significant receivables and inventory, a borrowing base certificate determines how much the borrower can draw on the line at any given time. The eligible borrowing base is typically calculated as 80 to 85 percent of eligible accounts receivable and 50 percent of eligible inventory, with exclusions for aged receivables, concentration limits, and ineligible inventory categories. A front-end banker needs to understand this well enough to explain it and to recognize when an asset-based structure is the right fit.

Global cash flow analysis:

For business owners who are also personally guaranteeing, credit will analyze global cash flow, all sources and uses of cash across both the business and the personal balance sheet. A business that looks fine on its own may look different when the owner's personal debt obligations, other business interests, and personal living expenses are added in. Ask the global cash flow question before submission.

Industry benchmarks, know them before you submit:

C&I underwriting is more industry-specific than real estate lending. A 45-day receivables balance is healthy for a manufacturer but concerning for a medical practice. Before submitting a C&I deal, know the relevant benchmarks for the industry, typical margins, normal receivables aging, expected inventory turns. The goal isn't to perform a full ratio analysis. It's to recognize when the business's numbers look unusual relative to its industry and to ask why before credit does.

What credit will look for:

✓ Cash flow durability, not just current performance, typically three years of history to assess whether earnings are stable, growing, or declining

✓ Clear purpose and use of proceeds, specific connection between the loan and a measurable improvement in cash flow capacity

✓ Line behavior and repayment history, does the line revolve? Does it pay down seasonally? Has it been fully drawn for extended periods?

✓ Owner compensation and distributions, consistent, reasonable draws reconciled against business profitability

✓ Key-person risk, whether the business could survive the loss of the owner or a key employee, and whether that risk is addressed

Where these deals die:

⚠️ Operating cycle not understood, line is sized to a round number rather than the actual cash gap

⚠️ Permanently drawn line presented as working capital need, structural mismatch not identified before submission

⚠️ Global cash flow not analyzed, guarantor has personal obligations that break coverage when added to the business picture

⚠️ Industry benchmarks not checked, anomalies in the financials not identified before credit asks about them

⚠️ One-year performance presented as a pattern, one strong year preceded by two weak ones doesn't support the story

⚠️ Use of proceeds is vague, "general working capital" invites credit questions that should have been answered at the front end

⚠️ Key-person risk identified but unaddressed, no life or disability insurance, no succession plan, no depth below the owner

Discovery questions, ask before the file is half-built:

→ Walk me through a typical operating cycle, from when you spend money to when you collect it.

→ What does the line look like at its peak balance, and what does it look like at its lowest point each year?

→ Has the line ever fully paid down to zero? If not, what's the lowest it's been in the last two years?

→ What does this equipment do that the business can't do now, or can't do as efficiently? (For equipment loans.)

→ How did you arrive at the purchase price, and have you reviewed the last three years of tax returns against it? (For acquisitions.)

→ What is the seller's role going to be after closing, and for how long?

→ Outside of this business, do you have other significant financial obligations I should know about?

→ What does a bad year look like for this business, specifically, what causes revenue to drop and how does the business respond?

→ Are there any major changes coming, ownership, management, customers, competition, that I should understand?

A Note on Using These Chapters

These four chapters are not a substitute for your institution's credit policy, SBA standard operating procedures, or the judgment of experienced colleagues. They are a starting point, the minimum a front-end banker should know before having the first substantive conversation about any of these loan types.

The banker who reads Chapter 10 before sitting down with their first construction borrower will ask better questions, identify risks earlier, and submit a more complete file than the one who learns the mechanics after the deal is half-built. That's the point.

> ***Know the instrument before you use it. The borrower is counting on it.***

CHAPTER 13

The Front-End Process Flow

Commercial lending doesn't start with a credit memo.

It starts with a conversation.

By the time a deal reaches underwriting, most of the outcome has already been determined, not by ratios or policy, but by how well the opportunity was understood, framed, and structured at the front end. The credit memo is largely a record of decisions already made.

This chapter walks through what actually happens between first contact and credit review, and where bankers make the biggest difference. Think of it as the path from raw opportunity to credit-ready deal.

Step One: The Initial Conversation

Every commercial loan begins the same way, with a borrower explaining why they need money.

At this stage, their explanation is almost always incomplete, simplified, and framed around urgency. That's normal. Borrowers experience their problems from the inside. They don't always have the language or the distance to describe them clearly.

Your job in the initial conversation is not to judge or decide. It's to listen for clues: What problem are they actually trying to solve? Is this about timing, growth, stress, or transition? Does the request sound temporary or permanent?

> ***The first version of a loan request is rarely the right one. Good bankers treat it as a starting point, not a proposal.***

Step Two: Discovery, Not Selling

Discovery is where lending actually begins.

This is where you slow the process down, just enough to understand what's really happening inside the business. Good discovery focuses on how the business makes money, where cash gets tight, what's changed recently, and what the owner is worried about but hasn't said yet.

You are not collecting data for a spreadsheet. You are building a mental model of the business, one that will inform every structural decision that follows.

Discovery is also where you begin to see whether the issue is structural or temporary, whether debt is actually the right solution, and whether the timing helps or hurts the request.

> ***Discovery done well saves everyone time later. Discovery skipped creates problems that compound.***

Step Three: Framing the Real Request

Once you understand the business, you can reframe the request, often back to the borrower themselves.

This might sound like: "What you really need is flexibility during your busy season." Or: "This looks more like an asset-financing need than working capital." Or: "Part of this request is long-term, and part is short-term, and they probably need to be structured differently."

Borrowers often feel relieved when someone helps them clarify the problem. They may not have the language, or the distance, to do it themselves. When a banker reframes a request well, it builds trust immediately.

Framing is not selling. It's translation. And it's where many deals either improve dramatically, or quietly fall apart.

Step Four: Shaping Structure

With the real need clarified, structure starts to take shape.

This is where you begin working through the core questions: How much is actually needed? How long should the bank be exposed? How does repayment align with cash flow? What risks need to be managed upfront?

It's also where creativity lives, splitting needs into multiple structures, right-sizing instead of maximizing, choosing discipline over convenience, phasing funding instead of committing everything at once.

At this stage, you're not finalizing terms. You're testing whether a reasonable structure exists at all. If it doesn't, that's valuable information, not failure. A deal that can't be structured soundly at the front end will only become harder to fix later.

Step Five: Pressure-Testing the Deal

Before anything goes to credit, good bankers pressure-test the structure.

The questions are simple but important: What if revenue dips? What if growth slows? What if a key customer leaves? What if the owner gets distracted or pulls back?

You are not looking for perfection. You are looking for *fragility*.

Weak spots discovered at this stage can usually be fixed: adjusted amounts, different amortization, added structure, phased funding, SBA support. Weak spots discovered after closing are far harder and more expensive to address.

> ***The front end is the cheapest place to fix a problem. Take advantage of it.***

Step Six: Preparing the Deal for Credit

When a deal is ready for credit, it should be clear, not clever.

A well-prepared front-end deal answers five things plainly: who the borrower is, why the loan exists, how it gets repaid, where the risks are, and how structure manages those risks.

Notice what's missing from that list: advocacy, sales language, overconfidence. Credit doesn't need persuasion. It needs clarity. The banker's job at this stage is to make the reviewer's job easy, not to make a case.

When credit pushes back, it's almost always because something upstream wasn't fully resolved. That's feedback, not resistance. The right response is curiosity, not frustration.

Step Seven: Credit Review Is a Checkpoint, Not a Verdict

Many bankers treat credit like a finish line. It isn't.

Credit review is a checkpoint: Does the structure make sense? Are risks acknowledged honestly? Is the bank being appropriately compensated for uncertainty? Can this loan live quietly on the books for its full term?

Good credit conversations feel collaborative because the heavy thinking has already been done at the front end. When credit asks for changes, the right question isn't "why are they pushing back?" It's "what is the structure still missing?"

> ***Credit review is not where deals go to be approved. It's where deals go to be confirmed.***

Step Eight: Communicating Back to the Borrower

How you communicate the outcome matters as much as the outcome itself.

When a deal is approved as structured, reinforce why it works and set expectations early. When it's approved with changes, explain the logic, not the policy, and tie the changes to risk and sustainability. When it's declined, be honest, be respectful, and be specific about what would need to change.

Borrowers remember how they were treated, especially when the answer is no. A well-handled decline often leads to a stronger deal later. A poorly-handled approval can damage a relationship that should have been built on clarity.

Where Bankers Add the Most Value

Across all eight steps, bankers add the most value when they slow things down early, ask uncomfortable but necessary questions, resist the pull toward overstructuring, fix problems before they become terms, and treat credit as a partner rather than an obstacle.

> ***Most problem loans don't start with bad intentions. They start with rushed framing.***

Speed feels productive. But at the front end of commercial lending, speed is usually what turns a fixable problem into an unfixable one.

A Simple Way to Think About the Process

The entire front-end process can be understood through three lenses:

- **Understanding**, What's really happening in this business?
- **Structuring**, Can this risk be shaped into something workable?
- **Confirming**, Does this hold up under honest scrutiny?

If you skip the first two, the third becomes painful. Every frustrating credit conversation traces back to something that wasn't fully resolved in understanding or structuring.

A Final Front-End Discipline

Before sending any deal forward, ask yourself:

> ***If I were on the credit side, what question would I ask first? Then answer it, before they have to.***

That's the difference between pushing deals and building them.

Front-end commercial lending is not about speed. It's about quality. When the front end is done well, credit moves faster, borrowers feel understood, loans perform better, and problems surface earlier. The process isn't complicated, but it is intentional.

In the next chapter, we'll bring the process to life with common front-end deal patterns, the requests bankers hear most often, where they typically go wrong, and how good structure fixes them before they ever reach underwriting.

CHAPTER 14

The Full Arc: A CRE Deal, End-to-End

Everything in this book has been about principles. This chapter is about practice.

What follows is a complete walkthrough of a real-world deal type, an owner-occupied commercial real estate loan for a small restaurant owner. The names and details are composite, but the dynamics are genuine. Every pattern, warning sign, structural decision, and conversation moment reflects what actually happens at the front end of commercial lending.

Read it the first time for the story. Read it a second time for the teaching moments, which are marked throughout. By the end, you should be able to see how every concept from the preceding chapters connects in a single living deal.

The Setup

Maria Reyes has owned and operated a fast-casual Mexican restaurant, Cocina Reyes, for eleven years. The restaurant seats 60 indoors, does strong lunch and dinner volume, and has built a loyal neighborhood following. For the past six years, she's leased her space in a small strip mall. The lease has two years left.

Maria's landlord recently told her he's selling the strip mall. The new owner may want to redevelop. Maria is worried. She's built her entire business around this location, the foot traffic, the parking, the visibility. Moving would mean starting over in ways she's not sure she'd survive.

A commercial real estate broker she knows mentioned that a freestanding building two blocks away, a former dry cleaner, just came on the market. It's roughly the same square footage, needs some work, but is in the same neighborhood. The asking price is $680,000.

Maria calls her banker.

STAGE ONE

The Initial Conversation

The call lasts about twenty minutes. Maria explains the situation quickly, her lease, the potential sale, the building she found. She's clearly anxious, and her ask comes early:

> **Maria:** *"I need to buy a building. I think I found the right one. Can you help me figure out if I can afford it?"*

Her banker, Daniel, listens without interrupting. When Maria finishes, he doesn't answer her question directly. Instead, he asks one of his own.

> **Daniel:** *"Before we get into numbers, help me understand what's really driving this. Is this about the specific building, or is it about getting out of your lease situation?"*

Maria pauses. Then:

> **Maria:** *"Both, I think. But mostly the lease. I can't keep running a restaurant where I don't control the space."*

Daniel notes this. The primary motivation isn't the building, it's occupancy security. That distinction will matter when he structures the deal.

> **TEACHING MOMENT →** *The first version of a loan request is rarely the right one. Maria asked about affordability. What she actually needs is a conversation about risk, specifically, the risk of staying in her current situation versus the risk of buying. Daniel's opening question surfaces the real driver without making Maria feel interrogated.*

STAGE TWO

Discovery

Daniel schedules a longer call for two days later. Before it, he reviews what he knows: Cocina Reyes has been a deposit customer for four years. The account shows consistent cash flow, some seasonality (slower in January and February), and no overdrafts. He pulls the last two years of statements and makes some notes.

On the call, he works through the business before touching the real estate.

> **Daniel:** *"Tell me how the restaurant makes money on a typical week. Walk me through it like I've never been inside."*

Maria describes the operation: lunch is the volume driver, dinner is the margin driver, weekends run about 30% higher than weekdays. Labor is her biggest cost. Food cost has been creeping up. She has two part-time employees who've been with her for years and would leave if she moved.

> **Daniel:** *"What does a slow month look like versus a good month?"*
>
> **Maria:** *"Good month, maybe $85,000 in revenue. Slow month, January, February, closer to $52,000. But expenses don't move much. January is always tight."*
>
> **Daniel:** *"And right now, what's your rent?"*
>
> **Maria:** *"$4,800 a month. Which is why I'm nervous, the new owner will probably want more."*

Daniel asks about her savings, what she has available for a down payment, and whether she's looked at any other buildings. Maria has about $95,000 in a business savings account and another $40,000 in personal savings she'd be willing to use. She hasn't looked at other buildings, she's fixated on this one.

TEACHING MOMENT → *Discovery is about building a mental model of the business, not collecting data for a spreadsheet. Daniel now knows: the operating cycle, the seasonality pattern, the cost structure, the current lease obligation, and the available equity. He also knows something important about Maria's psychology: she's emotionally attached to a single solution. That's worth keeping in mind.*

STAGE THREE

The First Warning Sign

After the discovery call, Daniel pulls up the property listing Maria sent him. He runs some quick numbers.

The building is $680,000. At standard owner-occupied CRE terms, a 25-year amortization, 10-year maturity, 20% down, the loan would be $544,000. At a rate around 7.25%, the monthly payment would be approximately $3,870.

On the surface, that looks better than her current rent of $4,800. Maria mentioned this herself on the call: "The payment might actually be less than what I'm paying now."

But Daniel slows down. He does a few things Maria hasn't done.

First, he adds back the costs that come with ownership but not with leasing: property taxes (approximately $7,200/year in the area), insurance ($3,600/year), and a basic maintenance reserve ($4,800/year). That's an additional $1,300/month on top of the loan payment. Total occupancy cost: approximately $5,170/month.

Second, he factors in the renovation. Maria mentioned the building "needs some work." He doesn't know how much yet, but that phrase is a flag. Dry cleaner conversions often involve environmental remediation, ventilation upgrades, and full kitchen buildouts. He's seen those run $150,000 to $300,000 for restaurant conversions.

Third, he looks at her slow months. At $52,000 in January revenue, after food cost (roughly 32%), labor (roughly 34%), and occupancy, her cash position gets tight. The loan payment is manageable in good months. In January, it's a different conversation.

> **TEACHING MOMENT →** *The comparison of "loan payment vs. rent" is one of the most common front-end traps in owner-occupied CRE. Borrowers almost always make it. The banker's job is to replace that comparison with a complete occupancy cost picture, including taxes, insurance, maintenance, and any renovation financing. Maria's deal looks different when all of those numbers are in the model.*

> ***Real estate should support the business, not constrain it. The banker's job is to find out which one this is before the borrower falls in love with the answer.***

STAGE FOUR

Reframing the Request

Daniel calls Maria back. He walks her through what he's found. He doesn't lead with problems, he leads with the full picture.

> **Daniel:** *"I want to show you what I'm seeing so we can make sure the structure actually works for the restaurant, not just on paper. The payment looks good against your current rent, but there are costs that come with ownership that aren't in your rent right now. And the renovation is a number I don't have yet, which is the one that concerns me most."*

Maria is quiet for a moment.

> **Maria:** *"I hadn't thought about the taxes and insurance separately. I guess I assumed those were included somehow."*

Daniel: *"A lot of people do. Here's how I'd like to think about this: before we go any further on this building, can we get a contractor in to look at the renovation scope? Because that number changes the whole conversation."*

Maria: *"How much do you think it could be?"*

Daniel: *"I've seen dry-cleaner-to-restaurant conversions run anywhere from $150,000 to $300,000. If it's on the lower end, this deal probably works. If it's on the higher end, we need to think carefully about whether you're taking on too much at once."*

Maria gets a contractor estimate two weeks later. The number comes back at $195,000 for the full buildout, including a ventilation system, kitchen equipment, flooring, and a small dining room refresh. Better than the worst case. But it changes the deal significantly.

> **TEACHING MOMENT →** *Reframing is not delivering bad news. It's completing the picture. Daniel doesn't tell Maria the deal won't work, he tells her what he needs to know before he can say it will. That's a different conversation, and it keeps Maria as a collaborative partner rather than putting her on the defensive.*

STAGE FIVE

Shaping the Structure

With the renovation number in hand, Daniel now has a complete picture of what Maria actually needs:

- **$680,000**, building purchase price
- **$195,000**, renovation and buildout
- **$875,000**, total project cost

Her available equity: $95,000 business savings + $40,000 personal = $135,000.

Standard owner-occupied CRE requires 10–15% down on the real estate. On $680,000 that's $68,000–$102,000. She can cover that. But the renovation is a separate need, and it can't be folded into the real estate loan without a construction component that complicates the deal and extends the timeline.

Daniel considers three structural paths.

Option A: Conventional Owner-Occupied CRE + Separate Construction Loan

Real estate loan: $612,000 (90% of $680,000), 25-year amortization, 10-year maturity. Construction loan: $195,000, converting to a 7-year term loan after buildout. Total debt service: approximately $6,100/month.

Problem: Combined debt service plus ownership costs pushes total occupancy to roughly $6,700/month. In a slow month, that's unsustainable.

Option B: SBA 504 Loan

An SBA 504 splits the financing: a conventional first mortgage at 50% of the project cost, an SBA debenture at 40%, and the borrower contributing 10%. For Maria's $875,000 project, that's a $437,500 first mortgage, a $350,000 SBA debenture, and an $87,500 borrower contribution.

The SBA portion amortizes over 25 years at a fixed rate, which significantly reduces payment pressure. Total monthly debt service on a 504 structure: approximately $5,200, $5,400, inclusive of both loans.

This brings total occupancy cost (debt service plus taxes, insurance, maintenance) to approximately $6,500/month, still higher than current rent, but more manageable across seasonal variation.

Option C: SBA 7(a) for the Full Project

An SBA 7(a) can finance the full project up to $5 million. With 10% down ($87,500), the loan would be $787,500, amortized over 25 years. Monthly payment: approximately $5,600.

Total occupancy cost: approximately $6,900/month. Higher than Option B, but a single loan with a single closing. Simpler, but more expensive monthly.

TEACHING MOMENT → *This is the moment where SBA stops being a product and becomes a structuring tool. Maria's deal doesn't work cleanly under conventional financing, not because she's a weak credit, but because the renovation need creates a gap that conventional structure can't bridge without creating unsustainable payment pressure. SBA solves the structural mismatch. That's exactly what it's designed for.*

> ***SBA expands options. It doesn't change the rules of credit. The deal still has to work on real cash flow, not program optimism.***

STAGE SIX

Pressure-Testing the Deal

Daniel runs the SBA 504 structure through the restaurant's financials. He uses two scenarios: a normal month and a slow month.

Normal month (August): $78,000 revenue. After food cost (32%), labor (34%), and other operating expenses (12%), net operating income before occupancy is approximately $17,200. Occupancy cost under SBA 504: $6,500. That leaves $10,700 for debt service, owner compensation, and reserves. Workable.

Slow month (January): $52,000 revenue. After food cost, labor, and operating expenses, net operating income before occupancy is approximately $8,900. Occupancy cost: $6,500. That leaves $2,400. Tight. Not crushing, but tight.

Daniel runs one more scenario: what if the renovation goes 15% over budget? That adds roughly $29,000 to the project, which at SBA terms adds about $175/month to debt service. January still works, barely.

He also asks himself: what happens if Maria loses a key employee? Her two long-tenured part-timers were mentioned early in discovery. If one leaves, she's likely looking at higher turnover labor costs during a transition. He factors in a 3% labor increase and reruns the numbers. January becomes a loss month.

> **TEACHING MOMENT →** *Pressure-testing is not about finding reasons to decline. It's about finding the specific scenario where the deal breaks, so you can either fix the structure or have an honest conversation with the borrower. Daniel found his answer: the deal is fragile in January if any second variable moves against Maria at the same time. That's not a dealbreaker. It's a conversation.*

STAGE SEVEN

The Hard Conversation

Daniel calls Maria. He's going to recommend the SBA 504 structure, but he has one condition to discuss first.

> **Daniel:** *"I've run through the numbers a few different ways. The 504 structure works for this deal, I think it's the right path. But I want to be honest with you about what I'm seeing in January."*
>
> **Maria:** *"What do you mean?"*
>
> **Daniel:** *"Your slow months are tight. Not impossible, but tight. If January hits and something else goes sideways at the same time, a repair, a labor issue, a rough week, you're going to feel it. I want to make sure we build something into the structure that gives you a cushion."*
>
> **Maria:** *"Like what?"*
>
> **Daniel:** *"Two things. First, I'd like you to keep a minimum of $30,000 in operating reserves once you close. That's roughly six weeks of occupancy cost, it's your buffer for a slow January. Second, I want to talk about the renovation timeline. The sooner you're open in the new space, the sooner the revenue recovers. If the buildout runs long, you're carrying dual costs, your current lease and the new loan. Have you thought about that window?"*
>
> **Maria:** *"No. I assumed I'd close the restaurant for a few weeks during the move."*

Daniel: *"That's fine if it's a few weeks. But if the renovation runs four to six months, which is possible, you need to either negotiate a lease extension on your current space or have enough cash to carry both. Which do you think is more realistic?"*

This stops Maria. She hadn't thought through the transition period at all. They spend the next twenty minutes working through the timeline, and Maria agrees to approach her current landlord about a month-to-month extension while the renovation is underway.

TEACHING MOMENT → *The hard conversation is where front-end discipline earns trust. Daniel isn't trying to talk Maria out of the deal. He's making sure she walks in with her eyes open. A borrower who understands the risks before closing is a borrower who calls you early when something goes wrong, not after it's become a problem.*

> ***Borrowers remember how they were treated, especially in the moments that were inconvenient to be honest.***

STAGE EIGHT

Preparing the Deal for Credit

Daniel now assembles the deal for credit review. He organizes it around five questions he knows the credit team will ask.

1. Who is the borrower and what is the business?

Cocina Reyes, a single-location fast-casual restaurant with eleven years of operating history. Owner-operated. Consistent cash flow with predictable seasonality. No prior loan defaults or derogatory credit. Strong community presence and stable customer base.

2. Why does this loan exist?

Occupancy security. The borrower's current lease expires in two years, and the building is being sold to a developer. The business has operated at this location for eleven years; relocation risk is real and material. The proposed purchase eliminates that risk and reduces long-term occupancy cost relative to market lease rates in the area.

3. How does the loan get repaid?

Restaurant operating cash flow. Average monthly NOI before occupancy: approximately $13,500 (trailing 12-month average across seasonal variation). Total monthly occupancy cost post-closing: $6,500. Debt service coverage ratio: approximately 1.42x on average months, 1.10x in slowest months. Borrower maintaining $30,000 operating reserve as condition of approval.

4. Where are the risks and how is structure managing them?

Primary risks: renovation cost overrun, transition period (dual lease/loan carrying cost), and January seasonality. Mitigants: renovation bid in hand with 15% contingency modeled; month-to-month lease extension negotiated with current landlord; operating reserve requirement; SBA 504 structure reduces monthly payment pressure vs. conventional financing.

5. What does the structure look like?

SBA 504: $437,500 conventional first mortgage (50%), $350,000 SBA debenture (40%), $87,500 borrower equity (10%). Total project cost $875,000 including $195,000 renovation. Personal guarantee from Maria Reyes. Collateral: first lien on real property.

> **TEACHING MOMENT →** *Notice what's missing from this credit summary: advocacy, optimism, and sales language. Daniel isn't arguing for the deal, he's presenting it. The risks are named. The mitigants are specific. The structure is explained. Credit doesn't need persuasion. It needs clarity.*

> ***A well-prepared front-end deal answers five questions plainly. When credit has to ask those questions themselves, it means the front end wasn't finished.***

STAGE NINE

Credit Review and the One Pushback

Credit comes back with one question: they want to understand the renovation contractor. Is this a fixed-price contract or an estimate? If it's an estimate, they want a higher contingency reserve, they'd like to see 20% rather than 15%, which adds about $39,000 to the project.

Daniel calls Maria. She's frustrated.

> **Maria:** *"The contractor has done four restaurant buildouts. He's not guessing."*
>
> **Daniel:** *"I hear you. And I believe you. But credit is asking a structural question, not a character question. They're asking: if the renovation runs over, does the deal still work? The answer right now is 'barely.' They want it to be 'yes.'"*
>
> **Maria:** *"So what does that mean? Do I have to put more money in?"*
>
> **Daniel:** *"You have two options. You can increase your equity contribution by $39,000, which you have the savings to do. Or we can look at whether the contractor will provide a fixed-price contract, which removes the uncertainty entirely. Which feels more realistic to you?"*

Maria calls the contractor. He agrees to a fixed-price contract with a defined change order process. Daniel sends the updated information to credit. The deal is approved.

TEACHING MOMENT → *Credit pushback is almost never arbitrary. When credit asks a question, it's because something in the structure is still carrying unresolved risk. Daniel's job here isn't to argue with credit, it's to translate their concern into an action Maria can take. The deal didn't change. The uncertainty did.*

STAGE TEN

Communicating the Outcome

Daniel calls Maria with the approval.

> **Daniel:** *"We're approved. I want to walk you through the terms so nothing surprises you at closing."*

He goes through the structure: the two-loan 504 arrangement, the payment schedule, the personal guarantee, the operating reserve requirement, and the reporting expectations (annual financial statements, quarterly revenue updates for the first two years).

> **Maria:** *"The quarterly updates, is that normal?"*

> **Daniel:** *"For a first two years post-renovation, yes. It's not because anyone is worried, it's because you're going through a significant transition and we want to stay close. If everything looks good at the two-year mark, we'll move to annual. Think of it as a check-in, not a review."*

> **Maria:** *"That's fair. Honestly, I'd want to know if something was going sideways anyway."*

Daniel also walks her through the transition plan one more time: the month-to-month extension, the renovation timeline, the reopening target. Maria has a clear picture of what the next six months look like. She knows what to watch for. She knows when to call.

TEACHING MOMENT → *The approval conversation is not the finish line. It's the handoff from deal-making to relationship management. How the terms are explained at closing determines whether the borrower calls the banker early when something changes, or waits until it's too late.*

What Made This Deal Work

Cocina Reyes is not a complicated credit. Eleven years of operating history, consistent cash flow, a motivated borrower with real equity. But deals like this fail at the front end more often than you'd expect, not because the credit is weak, but because the structure was never thought through.

Here's what Daniel did that made the difference:

- He asked about the motivation before discussing the numbers. The difference between "I want this building" and "I need occupancy security" is a structural difference, not a cosmetic one.
- He completed the picture before Maria could fall in love with an incomplete one. The payment-vs-rent comparison is a trap. He disarmed it early.
- He used SBA as a structuring tool, not a fallback. The 504 wasn't a way to get a marginal deal done. It was the right instrument for the specific mismatch between Maria's equity and her total project cost.
- He named the fragile scenario before credit did. January was the weak spot. Naming it, modeling it, and building in a reserve turned a potential credit concern into a managed risk.
- He treated credit's pushback as information. The renovation contingency question wasn't an obstacle. It was a solvable problem that made the deal stronger.

- He didn't stop at approval. The closing conversation set Maria up to be a good borrower, one who calls early, reports honestly, and understands why the structure is what it is.

> ***Good loans don't happen by accident. They're built, one question, one honest conversation, one structural decision at a time.***

One Last Note

This deal closed. Cocina Reyes reopened in its new location fourteen weeks after the renovation began, two weeks ahead of schedule. The first January in the new space was tight, as expected. Maria used $11,000 of her operating reserve and rebuilt it by March.

At the two-year check-in, Daniel reviewed the financials. Revenue was up 12% over the prior location, the new space had better visibility and slightly more seating. The loan was performing without a single missed payment.

At the end of that call, Maria said something Daniel wrote down.

> **Maria:** *"I'm glad you made me slow down on this. I almost went to a different bank because I thought they'd just say yes faster. I'm glad I didn't."*

That's what front-end discipline looks like from the other side of the table.

CHAPTER 15

The Banker's Relationship with the Institution

Most of this book has been about the conversation across the table, between a banker and a borrower, shaping a deal that makes sense. The borrower's need is clear. The structure is sound. The cash flow supports it. The guarantor is strong.

And the loan still might not get made.

Not because it's a bad deal. Because it's the wrong deal for this institution.

This chapter is about a dimension of front-end lending that doesn't get enough attention: the fit between the deal and the institution being asked to make it. A loan that belongs on someone else's books is not a loan that belongs on yours. And part of your job as a front-end banker is to know the difference before you bring the deal to credit, not after.

Appetite Is Not the Same as Eligibility

Every institution has policies that define what it will lend on: eligible collateral, loan-to-value limits, minimum DSCR thresholds, maximum exposures by loan type and industry. Those policies set the floor. A deal that doesn't meet policy can't move forward.

But meeting policy is not the same as fitting the institution.

Appetite is the institution's actual willingness to do a particular type of deal, in a particular market, at a particular point in time. It is shaped by portfolio concentration, regulatory feedback, strategic priorities, leadership philosophy, and the collective memory of deals that performed and deals that didn't. Appetite changes. It is not always written down. And it is not always explained to the banker in the field.

> ***A deal can be clean, creditworthy, and well-structured, and still be the wrong deal for your institution right now. Knowing that before you build the relationship is part of the job.***

Common appetite mismatches: an institution that has pulled back from construction lending after a difficult cycle; one that has a concentration limit in a specific industry already near its ceiling; one that lacks the operational infrastructure to service a complex SBA transaction efficiently; one whose leadership has quietly decided to exit a geographic market or loan type that no longer fits the strategy.

None of those are written into the policy manual. But they are real. And the banker who doesn't know them brings deals that go nowhere, damages relationships with borrowers who were well-qualified, and spends time that could have been invested in deals that actually fit.

Experience Is Part of Appetite

Appetite isn't only about willingness. It's about competence.

A lender who has never underwritten a cannabis-adjacent business, a franchise resale, a medical practice acquisition, or a self-storage construction deal is not just unfamiliar with the deal type, they are unfamiliar with how it fails. They don't know which assumptions to stress-test, which covenants provide meaningful early warning, or which collateral positions are harder to liquidate than the appraisal suggests.

That gap in institutional experience is real, and it has consequences that compound over the life of the loan. Underwriting a deal your credit team has never seen before produces a credit memo that looks complete but is missing the questions that experience would have asked. Approving a deal your portfolio team has never managed produces a monitoring process that doesn't know what to watch for. And collecting on collateral your workout team has never handled produces recoveries that are slower, more expensive, and less complete than the model assumed.

> ***Every deal type carries institutional learning requirements. A lender can underwrite a loan type they've never seen. But they can't do it as well as one they have. And the gap between those two outcomes is paid by the portfolio.***

This is not an argument for institutional timidity. Growth requires doing things for the first time. But doing something for the first time with intention, with added oversight, appropriate conservatism in assumptions, and honest acknowledgment of the learning curve, is very different from doing it accidentally, in a deal where the banker didn't realize the institution was operating outside its experience base.

The Collection Problem

Here is a question that rarely gets asked at the front end: if this deal goes wrong, can this institution collect effectively?

It should be asked more often.

Collateral that looks strong on paper can be nearly impossible to liquidate for an institution that has no experience handling it. A restaurant with a liquor license and specialized equipment. A medical practice with receivables tied to billing codes and provider agreements. Specialized industrial machinery that requires a buyer who knows what it does. Self-storage facilities in markets the institution doesn't operate in.

The institution that has never taken back this type of collateral does not know what it costs to store, maintain, insure, or sell it. It does not know which markets have active buyers and which don't. It does not know which legal and regulatory processes apply to its disposition. It learns all of that in workout, at the worst possible time, under the worst possible conditions, with a borrower whose cooperation may be limited.

The deal that looks right at origination but ends in a collection experience the institution wasn't prepared for isn't just a credit problem. It is an institutional learning cost that was paid at full price.

How to Know What Your Institution Will and Won't Do

The practical implication of all of this is straightforward: know your institution before you build a pipeline.

Some of that knowledge is available in writing, credit policy, concentration limits, product guidelines. Read them. But most of it lives in conversations with credit officers, senior lenders, and leadership who have institutional memory that doesn't appear in any document.

The questions worth asking regularly: What deal types have been declining at a higher rate lately, and why? What industries is the institution actively trying to grow, and which ones is it quietly pulling back from? What loan types have produced the most portfolio stress in recent years? Has the institution had experience with this collateral type in workout, and how did it go?

Those conversations are not weakness. They are due diligence. The banker who knows this landscape brings deals that fit. The one who doesn't brings deals that don't, and wonders why they keep losing traction in credit.

When the Deal Is Right and the Institution Isn't

This is the hardest version of the conversation: you have a good borrower, a sound deal, and a clear structure, and you can see, honestly, that this institution is not the right lender for it.

That situation calls for directness with the borrower. Not every banker is positioned to have this conversation easily, but it is the right one. A borrower who is told clearly, "we're not the right fit for this, and here's why", walks away with accurate information and the respect of having been dealt with honestly. That borrower remembers. They may come back when the situation changes, or refer someone whose deal does fit.

The borrower who is strung along through a process that was never going to result in a yes, who discovers the misfit late in the relationship after sharing their financials and investing weeks of time, walks away with a different impression, and a different story to tell.

> ***Telling a borrower you're not the right institution for their deal is one of the most honest things a banker can say. It protects the borrower's time. It protects the institution's credibility. And it is almost always remembered more favorably than a late decline.***

Fit Is a Two-Sided Question

The framework in this book is built around shaping deals that work for both the borrower and the bank. That second half, for the bank, requires more than credit analysis. It requires honest institutional self-knowledge.

A good loan is one that makes sense for the borrower's business. A loan that belongs on your books is one that also makes sense for your institution's capacity, experience, and appetite. The best front-end bankers hold both of those standards at the same time.

When they align, the deal is ready. When they don't, even if the credit is strong, the right move is to say so early, clearly, and without apology.

"The loan is sound. But I don't think we're the right fit for it."

That sentence, said honestly and early, is not a failure. It is the front-end discipline working exactly as it should.

In the next chapter, we'll move into the patterns that repeat most often at the front end, the familiar deal shapes that arrive with different borrowers and different details but follow the same logic, and fail in the same ways.

Common Front-End Deal Patterns

After you've spent some time at the front end of commercial lending, you start to notice something important.

Most deals aren't unique.

They feel unique to the borrower. They sound unique in the first conversation. But structurally, they tend to fall into a handful of familiar patterns, and those patterns tend to fail in familiar ways.

Pattern recognition is one of the most valuable skills a banker can develop. It doesn't make lending mechanical. It makes it **thoughtful**. When you've seen a pattern enough times, you start asking better questions earlier, and fixing problems before they harden into terms or declines.

<u>Pattern One</u>: "We Just Need a Line of Credit"

This is the most common opening line in commercial lending. Sometimes it's correct. Often, it isn't.

What's Really Happening

The business is experiencing cash pressure, but the cause varies. It might be growth, seasonality, poor cash management, thin margins, or delayed collections. The borrower asks for a line because it feels flexible and noncommittal. But flexibility isn't always what the business needs.

Where This Pattern Goes Wrong

The line gets sized too large, never pays down, and quietly becomes permanent debt. Meanwhile, the real issue, profitability, structure, timing, goes unaddressed. The line masks the problem rather than solving it.

How Good Structure Fixes It

Good bankers ask: what is the line actually funding? Should part of this be term debt instead? Does this business need discipline, not flexibility? Often the right answer is a smaller line paired with a term loan, or a phased approach that forces the business to prove itself before credit expands.

> ***Lines should fund cycles, not cover gaps forever.***

<u>Pattern Two</u>: "This Loan Will Let Us Grow"

Growth-driven requests sound optimistic, and often they are. But optimism doesn't repay debt.

What's Really Happening

The business is expanding capacity, hiring ahead of revenue, taking on larger projects, or scaling faster than cash flow allows. The loan is meant to bridge the gap between investment and payoff.

Where This Pattern Goes Wrong

Growth assumptions are too aggressive. Cash flow lags longer than expected. Fixed debt payments arrive before new revenue does. Stress replaces momentum, and a loan that was supposed to accelerate the business starts to slow it down.

How Good Structure Fixes It

Good structure matches repayment to realistic timing, avoids front-loading payments, and uses the smallest amount necessary. Sometimes it phases funding, committing to the first stage before releasing the rest.

The key question isn't "will growth happen?" It's "can the business carry this debt *while* growth is happening?"

Pattern Three: "We Want to Refinance Existing Debt"

Refinancing requests are common, and often reasonable. But they require careful front-end thinking because they can go two very different directions.

What's Really Happening

Refinancing can mean simplification, lower payments, better structure, or quiet distress. The borrower may be solving a real problem, or postponing one. The difference matters enormously.

Where This Pattern Goes Wrong

Old problems get rolled forward. Short-term debt becomes long-term without fixing the underlying cause. Payment relief replaces discipline. And the bank inherits someone else's mess, often without realizing it until the loan seasons.

How Good Structure Fixes It

Good bankers ask three questions before agreeing to refinance: Why did the existing structure fail? What changes this time? What discipline is being added, not removed?

Refinancing should improve alignment, reduce fragility, and clarify repayment. If it only improves comfort, the structure isn't finished.

<u>Pattern Four</u>: "We're Buying Something"

Acquisitions, buyouts, and asset purchases are among the most complex front end requests, and among the most prone to structural gaps.

What's Really Happening

The business is making a long-term bet, changing its own structure, and taking on integration risk. Borrowers tend to focus on the purchase itself, the price, the terms, the opportunity. What comes after the close often gets less attention than it deserves.

Where This Pattern Goes Wrong

Cash flow is overestimated. Integration costs are ignored. Working capital needs are missed. Debt service arrives before the business has stabilized. What looked like a smart acquisition becomes a drain on an otherwise healthy operation.

How Good Structure Fixes It

Good structure separates purchase financing from operating needs, leaves room for integration friction, avoids maximum leverage, and builds in review points.

> ***Buying something is not the same as absorbing it. Structure should assume friction.***

<u>Pattern Five</u>: "We Own the Real Estate: So It's Safer"

Owner-occupied real estate often feels like a strong anchor. Sometimes it is. Sometimes it shifts risk rather than eliminates it.

What's Really Happening

The business is locking in occupancy, building equity, and increasing fixed costs. Each of those things has real value, but they also change the operating picture in ways borrowers don't always anticipate.

Where This Pattern Goes Wrong

Cash flow gets tighter. Flexibility disappears. Real estate starts to be used as the solution to unrelated operating problems, "we can always borrow against the building", and the business becomes asset-rich and cash-poor.

How Good Structure Fixes It

Good front-end structure keeps real estate sized conservatively, preserves operating flexibility, and resists using property to fix business issues that property can't actually fix.

Real estate should support operations, not constrain them.

Pattern Six: "SBA Will Make This Work"

SBA comes up most often when conventional structure feels tight. That's not a problem, but it requires discipline.

What's Really Happening

The business is short on equity, early in its lifecycle, growing unevenly, or structurally sound but constrained in ways conventional lending can't easily accommodate. SBA exists precisely for these situations.

Where This Pattern Goes Wrong

SBA gets used to justify weak fundamentals rather than solve structural ones. Longer amortization hides cash flow issues instead of giving the business room to grow into its obligations. Guarantees and structure get overlooked in the excitement of getting a deal done.

How Good Structure Fixes It

Good SBA deals solve structural mismatches, improve sustainability, and still rely on real repayment, not program optimism.

> ***SBA expands options. It doesn't change the rules of credit.***

Pattern Seven: "This Is a Relationship Deal"

Every banker hears this one. And it's the pattern that causes the most personal discomfort when it goes wrong.

What's Really Happening

The borrower has history with the bank, is well-liked, feels trusted, and may genuinely deserve that trust. Relationships matter, they provide context, build continuity, and often reflect real character. The problem is when relationship becomes a substitute for structure.

Where This Pattern Goes Wrong

Weak deals get approved. Structure softens in ways it shouldn't. Early warning signs get explained away rather than addressed. And when problems eventually surface, as they often do, they feel personal in a way that pure credit decisions never do.

How Good Structure Fixes It

Strong relationships deserve strong structure, not special treatment. The best banking relationships are built on clarity, consistency, and honest discipline.

> ***The clearest signal of a strong relationship is a borrower who respects your structure, not one who expects you to bend it.***

Why Patterns Matter

Recognizing patterns doesn't mean every deal fits neatly into a category. It means you arrive at each new conversation with the right questions already loaded.

When you know where these patterns typically break, you can structure around that risk from the start, before it shows up as a credit concern, a problem credit, or an awkward conversation with a borrower who didn't see it coming.

That's not pessimism. That's experience in usable form.

A Front-End Habit to Build

When a new deal appears, ask yourself: which pattern does this resemble, and where do those deals usually break?

> ***Then structure around that risk. Every time.***

Most front-end deals don't fail because they're bad ideas. They fail because familiar risks were ignored in the excitement of something that felt new. The goal of commercial lending isn't creativity for its own sake. It's recognizing what you've seen before, and structuring wisely.

In the next chapter, we'll shift perspective entirely and look at lending from the borrower's side, how structure feels from the other side of the table, where misunderstandings tend to form, and how great bankers communicate clarity without creating friction.

CHAPTER 17

How Borrowers Experience Structure

Bankers experience loans as structure.

Borrowers experience loans as **feelings**.

Relief. Pressure. Confusion. Confidence. Frustration. Those reactions don't come from interest rates or policy language. They come from how structure intersects with a borrower's day-to-day reality, the payroll they're covering, the slow month they're managing, the growth they're chasing.

This chapter shifts perspective. It looks at commercial lending from the other side of the table and explains why good structure often feels supportive while bad structure feels personal, even when it isn't. Understanding this helps bankers communicate better, anticipate resistance, and build stronger relationships without compromising discipline.

Borrowers Don't Experience "Structure", They Experience Constraints

Borrowers don't wake up thinking about amortization or maturity dates. They experience monthly payments, cash flow pressure, reporting requests, limits on flexibility, and periodic check-ins with the bank.

When structure fits the business, those things feel manageable, even helpful. When structure doesn't fit, borrowers feel boxed in, second-guessed, or misunderstood.

> ***Most borrower frustration is not about credit decisions. It's about misalignment.***

That distinction matters. A borrower who feels misunderstood isn't necessarily arguing against the bank, they're signaling that the structure hasn't been explained in terms that connect to how they actually run their business.

Why Good Structure Often Feels Tight at First

One of the most counterintuitive truths in commercial lending is this:

> ***Good structure often feels uncomfortable early, and comfortable later. Poor structure feels easy at first, then becomes painful.***

Early on, borrowers with well-structured loans may feel that payments are higher than expected, reporting feels intrusive, or limits feel unnecessarily restrictive. But over time, discipline tends to improve operations, cash flow becomes more predictable, stress decreases, and trust builds.

Poorly structured loans do the opposite. They feel flexible and accommodating at first. Then reality arrives, and pressure spikes in ways the borrower didn't anticipate and the bank can't easily fix.

Bankers who understand this can normalize early discomfort without apologizing for it. The right frame isn't "I'm sorry this feels tight", it's "this is designed to work in slow months, not just good ones."

Where Borrowers Commonly Misunderstand Structure

Most borrower confusion clusters around three recurring questions. Each one has a clear, honest answer, if the banker is willing to give it.

"Why Can't I Just Have More?"

Borrowers often see unused credit as safety. Banks see unused credit as potential risk. When limits exist, borrowers may feel constrained, but those limits exist to match debt to capacity, prevent overextension, and protect flexibility later.

The right explanation reframes limits as protection, not denial. A borrower who understands why a limit exists rarely fights it the same way.

"Why Does the Bank Care How I Use the Money?"

From the borrower's view, money feels fungible. From the bank's view, purpose defines repayment. When structure ties funds to specific uses, it's not about control, it's about alignment.

Borrowers who genuinely understand this tend to make better decisions *with* the bank instead of around it. That's worth taking time to explain.

"Why Do You Need My Financials Again?"

To borrowers, reporting can feel repetitive and intrusive. To banks, time without information is risk. The best bankers explain reporting as a shared dashboard, a way to spot issues early, before they become problems that require harder conversations.

When reporting is framed as a partnership tool rather than a surveillance mechanism, resistance drops significantly.

Borrowers Feel Structure Through Cash Flow

More than anything else, borrowers experience structure through cash flow pressure.

They don't think in terms of debt service coverage ratios or amortization schedules. They think in terms of: can I make payroll? Do I have room to operate? What happens if this month is slow?

When structure matches cash flow, borrowers feel supported. When it fights cash flow, they feel trapped, even if the loan is technically performing.

> ***Borrowers live inside the loan every day. The front end is the only chance to make sure it fits.***

Guarantees Feel Personal: Even When They Aren't

From the bank's perspective, guarantees are alignment tools. From the borrower's perspective, they're deeply personal.

Guarantees touch identity, risk tolerance, family security, and pride. A business owner signing a personal guarantee isn't just agreeing to a legal term, they're putting their name on the line in a way that feels different from any other part of the transaction.

Bankers who ignore this emotional layer often create friction that didn't need to exist. The key isn't to avoid guarantees, it's to explain them in a way that lands correctly: as shared commitment, as confidence in the business, as a signal that both sides are aligned.

When guarantees are framed as punishment, trust erodes. When framed as alignment, they're often accepted without much resistance at all.

Why Borrowers Push Back on "Reasonable" Terms

When borrowers push back, it's rarely about the term itself.

It's usually about fear, fear of losing flexibility, fear of future surprises, fear of being locked into something that won't work if circumstances change. Good bankers listen for the emotion underneath the objection rather than treating it as a negotiation to win.

Pushback often reveals something worth knowing: a misunderstood cash cycle, an unspoken concern about a specific scenario, or a structural mismatch that deserves a second look.

> ***Resistance is information, not defiance. The banker who hears it that way finds better structure. The banker who doesn't creates unnecessary friction.***

The Borrower's Mental Model of the Bank

Borrowers tend to see banks in one of three ways: as a partner, as a necessary evil, or as a last resort.

Partners experience the bank as a source of clear expectations, consistent behavior, and predictable structure. Necessary evils see the bank as transactional, rigid, and reactive, something to deal with, not work with. Last resorts only approach the bank under stress, which means the relationship starts in the worst possible context.

Front-end structure largely determines which model forms. When structure is thoughtful and explained well, borrowers almost always move toward partnership, even when terms are firm. The terms aren't the obstacle. The explanation is.

How Great Bankers Communicate Structure

The best bankers don't overwhelm borrowers with detail. They explain *why* before *what*, tie structure to the borrower's own goals, normalize discipline, and avoid defensive language.

In practice, that sounds like: "This structure gives you room where you need it." Or: "These terms help us spot issues early, not punish you." Or: "This is designed to work in slow months, not just good ones."

Borrowers don't need to love structure. They need to understand it. That's a lower bar than most bankers realize, and a higher bar than most bankers consistently clear.

When Borrower Discomfort Is a Warning Sign

Not all discomfort is bad. But some of it matters in a different way.

Pay close attention when borrowers resist any accountability, want flexibility without any limits, avoid discussing downside scenarios, or treat structure as negotiable decoration rather than functional design.

Those reactions often signal deeper issues: unrealistic cash flow assumptions, low tolerance for actual risk, or a misalignment in what the borrower expects the loan to do. That's not a communication problem, it's a structural signal.

Bankers should receive it as useful information, not a negotiation challenge to overcome.

A Simple Empathy Check

Before finalizing any structure, ask yourself:

> ***If I ran this business, how would this loan feel on my worst month, not my best one?***

If the answer is "manageable but firm," you're probably close. If the answer is "crushing," the structure needs more work. If the answer is "irrelevant," the loan may not be solving the right problem.

Borrowers don't experience lending the way bankers do. They experience it through daily decisions, monthly pressure, and emotional reactions that don't show up in financial statements.

Bankers who understand this don't soften structure. They **explain it better**. That's how discipline and trust coexist.

In the next chapter, we'll bring the front-end perspective to its final test: identifying early warning signs before credit ever sees them, and knowing when the best loan decision is to slow down, restructure, or wait.

CHAPTER 18

Front-End Warning Signs

Most problem loans don't start with bad intentions.

They start with small signals that were easy to ignore.

Front-end warning signs are rarely dramatic. They don't announce themselves as credit issues. They show up as discomfort, vagueness, urgency, or optimism that doesn't quite line up with reality. And because they're easy to explain away, especially when a borrower is likable and the story sounds good, they often go unaddressed until they've hardened into terms, declines, or problem credits.

This chapter is about learning to recognize those signals early. The goal isn't to become suspicious of every borrower. It's to become observant.

> ***Good bankers don't eliminate risk. They recognize it early enough to manage it.***

Warning Signs Are About Pattern, Not Proof

At the front end, you are not proving anything. You are noticing patterns.

A single red flag rarely means much on its own. A cluster of them usually does. Warning signs matter not because they guarantee failure, but because they tell you where structure needs to work harder, or where timing may simply be wrong.

With that framing in mind, here are the ten most common front-end warning signs.

Warning Sign #1: Urgency Without Clarity

Urgency isn't automatically bad. Businesses operate under real deadlines, and sometimes timing genuinely matters. But urgency without a clear explanation is a signal worth following.

Listen carefully when borrowers say they need this done quickly, that timing is critical, or that they can't wait. Then ask: what happens if this doesn't close now? What changed recently? Why now instead of six months ago?

Healthy urgency has a clear cause. Unhealthy urgency often masks stress, a payment due, a relationship strained, a decision that should have been made earlier. Good structure slows things down just enough to understand what's driving the rush.

Warning Sign #2: Vague Use of Proceeds

Borrowers should be able to explain what they're borrowing for. When they can't, or won't, pay attention.

Vague answers sound like "general business purposes," "working capital," or "flexibility." Those phrases aren't wrong on their own, but they're incomplete. Behind a vague use of proceeds is often multiple problems bundled together, cash flow uncertainty, or avoidance of details the borrower finds uncomfortable to discuss.

> ***Structure can't fix what isn't defined. When purpose stays fuzzy, structure will too.***

Warning Sign #3: Repayment Depends on "Next Year"

Optimism is not a repayment plan.

Be cautious when repayment relies on growth that hasn't happened yet, new customers not yet secured, cost savings not yet realized, or market conditions improving. Statements like "once we land this contract," "next year will be better," and "we're turning the corner" may be true, but structure should not depend on them.

Good loans work *before* improvement, not because of it. If a loan only makes sense after something positive happens, the timing may simply be wrong.

Warning Sign #4: Permanent Use of Temporary Tools

This warning sign shows up most often with lines of credit, and it's one of the easiest to miss because it doesn't look like a problem, it looks like stability.

Pay attention when lines are always fully drawn, balances never decline, or borrowers describe their line as "part of the capital structure." A permanently drawn line is a structural mismatch. A long-term need is being funded short-term. Discipline has eroded. Risk is being disguised as flexibility.

This isn't necessarily a decline signal, but it is a restructuring signal. The right move is to separate the need and address it honestly, not to keep renewing the same instrument that isn't doing the job it was designed for.

Warning Sign #5: Resistance to Basic Questions

Borrowers don't have to love every question. Some pushback is normal and healthy. But resistance to basic clarity is a different thing.

Watch for defensiveness around cash flow, discomfort discussing downside scenarios, dismissiveness toward structure, or frustration with transparency. These reactions often signal thin margins, fragile confidence, past issues not fully resolved, or a mismatch between what the borrower expects and what the bank will require.

> ***Good borrowers may push back, but they engage. Avoidance is the real signal.***

Warning Sign #6: Guarantees Doing All the Work

If a deal feels safe *only* because of a guarantor, pause.

Listen for phrases like "the guarantor is very strong," "worst case, they'll cover it," or "there's plenty of net worth." Strong guarantors are genuinely helpful, but they are not structure. When guarantees are carrying the deal, something more fundamental is missing: cash flow, right-sized debt, proper term, clear purpose.

Guarantees should reinforce structure, not replace it. A deal that only works because of a guarantor is a deal waiting for a problem.

Warning Sign #7: "This Is How We've Always Done It"

History is useful context. It is not protection.

Be cautious when borrowers lean heavily on past success, long relationships, or familiar patterns as the primary reason a loan should work. Statements like "this has always worked," "we've never had an issue," or "the bank knows us" deserve a respectful but direct response: markets change, businesses evolve, and structure must keep up.

Past performance explains context. It doesn't eliminate forward-looking risk, and a banker who treats it as if it does will eventually be surprised by a borrower who wasn't.

Warning Sign #8: One Loan Trying to Solve Everything

When a single loan request tries to fund growth, fix cash flow, refinance old debt, buy assets, and create flexibility all at once, it's usually doing too much.

This is one of the most classic front-end mistakes, and it's easy to miss because the borrower's enthusiasm can make it feel like opportunity rather than overreach.

> ***Good structure simplifies. Bad structure bundles. When everything is rolled into one request, the right move is to slow down and separate needs, not to decline outright.***

Warning Sign #9: Borrower Focused Only on Approval

Some borrowers care deeply about structure, about whether the loan actually fits, whether the terms make sense, whether they'll be able to live with it. Others care only about getting to yes.

Be cautious when borrowers push for approval over fit, minimize discussion of terms, treat structure as an obstacle to work around, or resist changes that would clearly improve sustainability. These aren't just negotiating tactics, they're signals about how the borrower will behave once the loan is on the books.

Approval is an event. Structure is a relationship. Borrowers who understand that distinction tend to make better long-term partners.

Warning Sign #10: You Feel Uncomfortable, but Can't Explain Why

This is one of the most important signals of all, and the one most often dismissed.

Front-end discomfort is rarely random. It usually comes from incomplete information, misaligned structure, unanswered questions, or emotional pressure to move faster than the thinking justifies. When you feel uneasy but can't articulate why, that feeling deserves respect.

> ***Ask: what don't I understand yet? Discomfort is often your experience noticing something your words haven't caught up to yet.***

Don't talk yourself out of it. Sit with it long enough to name it. The answer will usually point directly at the next question to ask.

What to Do When You See Warning Signs

Warning signs are not reasons to stop. They are reasons to slow down, ask better questions, reframe the request, adjust structure, and consider timing.

Many strong loans start with warning signs, and end up well-structured precisely because someone noticed them early and did the work to address them before they became terms or declines.

Ignoring signals doesn't make deals better. Responding to them thoughtfully almost always does.

The Banker's Real Value

Bankers are not gatekeepers. They are translators, pattern-recognizers, and risk-shapers.

Your job at the front end isn't to avoid discomfort, it's to use it. The banker who gets comfortable with uncertainty, who treats unease as information rather than noise, is the one who builds deals that hold up.

A Final Front-End Discipline

Before moving any deal forward, ask yourself:

> ***If this loan becomes a problem, what will I wish I had asked today? Then ask it, now.***

Front-end warning signs are not about fear. They're about respect, for the borrower, for the bank, and for the long-term relationship that good structure makes possible.

When you learn to see them early, structure becomes easier, conversations become clearer, and outcomes improve quietly over time.

In the final chapter, we'll pull everything together, not as a checklist, but as a mindset you can carry into every commercial conversation going forward.

CHAPTER 19

Industry Patterns: How Cash Flows Differently

The same framework. Very different answers.

The front-end framework in this book is universal. The same five questions apply to every commercial deal, regardless of what the business does. The same structural principles hold whether you're looking at a restaurant or a manufacturer.

But the answers to those questions look very different depending on the industry. Cash flows differently. Seasonality patterns differently. Risk concentrates in different places. And the structural solutions that work for one type of business often don't work for another.

A banker who has seen thirty restaurant deals has a mental model for how restaurants work. They know what a healthy month looks like and what a stressed one looks like. They know where cash gets tight and why. They know which warning signs are specific to that type of business and which are universal.

A banker sitting across from their first restaurant doesn't have that yet. This chapter is a starting point.

> ***The goal is not to teach you everything about six industries. It's to show you the thinking process, so you can apply it to any industry you encounter, including ones not covered here.***

How to Use This Chapter

Each industry section follows the same structure: how money moves through the business, where cash pressure typically concentrates, structural considerations specific to the industry, and warning signs that are easy to miss if you don't know the pattern.

Read the industries most relevant to your current deal flow carefully. Read the others for the thinking pattern, because the questions you'll ask about a medical practice are the same ones you'll eventually ask about an industry not covered here.

At the end of this chapter, there's a framework for developing your own pattern recognition from scratch. That's the most transferable part of the whole chapter.

The Four Questions for Any Industry

Before diving into specific industries, it helps to have a consistent set of questions you'll ask regardless of the business type. These four questions surface the pattern in any industry:

- How does money come into this business, and how predictable is it?
- When does cash go out, and how does the timing of outflows relate to inflows?
- What causes cash pressure in this industry, seasonality, growth, concentration, something else?
- What does a stressed version of this business look like, and what usually causes it?

The answers to those four questions determine the right structure more reliably than any industry-specific rule. They are the questions that build pattern recognition over time.

Industry One: Restaurants and Food Service

High volume, thin margins, and a business that lives or dies on daily operations.

Industry Snapshot	
Cash cycle	Immediate, cash and card transactions settle daily
Typical margins	Net margins 3–8% in healthy operations; lower is common
Primary costs	Labor (30–35%), food cost (28–32%), occupancy (8–12%)
Seasonality	Varies by location; tourist-dependent operations highly seasonal
Common borrowing needs	Equipment, owner-occupied real estate, working capital, renovation
SBA fit	Strong, particularly for real estate and startup financing

How money moves

Restaurants are a cash-flow-today business. Unlike most commercial borrowers, restaurants collect revenue at the point of sale, every transaction settles immediately or within 24–48 hours for card payments. This means the operating cycle is short and cash conversion is fast.

The pressure isn't usually in receivables. It's in the gap between the fixed cost structure, rent, labor, utilities, loan payments, and the variable revenue that has to cover it. A slow week doesn't reduce the rent or the payroll. It just reduces the cash available to pay them.

Where cash pressure concentrates

The three pressure points in restaurant lending are occupancy cost, labor, and food cost. Of these, labor is the least flexible, a restaurant can't easily cut staff midweek and often can't reduce hours without affecting the customer experience that drives revenue. Food cost fluctuates with suppliers and menu mix but responds faster to management decisions than labor does.

Slow months are the key discovery question. In a healthy restaurant, slow months are uncomfortable but survivable. In a stressed one, slow months require outside cash, from a line, from reserves, or from the owner personally. The pattern of how slow months have been managed tells you more about the health of the business than the average month ever will.

Structural considerations

The most important structural question for a restaurant loan is the occupancy cost picture, and this matters whether the restaurant is leasing or buying. A loan payment that looks favorable against current rent may not look favorable when you add property taxes, insurance, and maintenance for an owned building. Always model the total occupancy cost, not just the debt service.

Location is collateral in a way that doesn't show up on a balance sheet. A restaurant's customer base is often attached to its physical location. A forced relocation, because of a lease not renewed, a landlord sale, or a failed real estate purchase, can reset the business to near-zero. Owner-occupied real estate for a restaurant isn't just an asset acquisition. It's an operational risk mitigation.

Watch for:

⚠️ Revenue tied to a single daypart (lunch only, dinner only), concentration risk

⚠️ Labor cost above 38% of revenue, often signals scheduling or turnover problems

⚠️ Food cost above 35% without a premium concept justification

⚠️ Owner who hasn't taken a salary for more than 12 months, the business may be subsidizing itself

⚠️ Lease with less than 3 years remaining and no renewal option, occupancy risk is real

⚠️ Multiple concepts or locations in rapid succession, execution risk before the first location is stable

Industry Two: Contractors and Trades

Cash goes out before it comes back, the operating cycle defines every structural decision.

Industry Snapshot	
Cash cycle	30–90 days from project start to collection; varies significantly
Typical margins	Net margins 5–12% depending on trade and market
Primary costs	Labor (35–45%), materials (25–35%), equipment and overhead
Seasonality	Strong in most markets, spring/summer peak, winter slow
Common borrowing needs	Working capital lines, equipment, vehicles, bonding support
SBA fit	Good for equipment and real estate; working capital lines typically conventional

How money moves

Contractors live inside the operating cycle more acutely than almost any other small business. They pay for materials upfront, pay labor weekly, and collect 30 to 90 days after work is complete, sometimes longer if the customer is a larger commercial entity with its own payment terms.

The cash gap between outflows and inflows is the fundamental driver of working capital needs in this industry. A contractor with $2M in annual revenue and 60-day receivables has roughly $330,000 in receivables outstanding at any given time, and all of it needs to be funded somehow. That's the structural need a line of credit exists to address.

Where cash pressure concentrates

Seasonal concentration is the most predictable pressure point. A contractor who does $180,000 in revenue in July may do $30,000 in January. The fixed costs, equipment payments, insurance, key employee salaries, don't adjust. The January cash position determines whether the business survives to the spring recovery.

The second pressure point is growth. A contractor who wins a significantly larger project than they've managed before suddenly needs more working capital than their line supports, more equipment than they own, and more management bandwidth than they've had to exercise. Growth is when contractor businesses most often run into trouble, not because the work isn't there, but because the operating infrastructure isn't ready for it.

Structural considerations

The working capital line for a contractor should be sized to the actual cash gap, which means the banker needs to understand the average receivables balance, the payment terms with major customers, and the seasonal pattern of cash flow. A line sized to the average month will be insufficient during peak season. A line sized to peak season will be permanently drawn during slow season.

Equipment financing for contractors is often straightforward, but the useful life question matters. A truck or piece of equipment financed over seven years that has a five-year useful life creates a structural mismatch, the business is paying for an asset that no longer generates revenue. Match amortization to realistic asset life, not to the borrower's preference for a lower payment.

Watch for:

⚠️ Receivables aging beyond 90 days, slow collections often precede cash flow stress

⚠️ Heavy concentration in one general contractor or one commercial client

⚠️ Equipment that's aging but not being replaced, deferred maintenance eventually becomes an emergency capital need

⚠️ Bonding limits that are close to capacity, signals the business is at or near its manageable project scale

⚠️ Owner as the only estimator, project manager, and relationship holder, key-person risk is high

⚠️ Working capital line that never pays down seasonally, structural mismatch, not a working capital need

Industry Three: Medical and Healthcare Practices

Stable demand, complex billing, and a cash cycle that depends on payers you don't control.

Industry Snapshot	
Cash cycle	45–120 days from service to collection depending on payer mix
Typical margins	Varies widely; primary care 10–18%, specialty 15–30%+
Primary costs	Labor (40–50%), occupancy, supplies, malpractice insurance
Seasonality	Mild, some practices see Q1 strength as deductibles reset
Common borrowing needs	Practice acquisition, equipment, real estate, working capital
SBA fit	Excellent, one of the strongest SBA borrower profiles when structured correctly

How money moves

Medical practices deliver services and then wait, sometimes a long time, to be paid. Unlike restaurants or retailers, healthcare practices rarely collect at the point of service. They submit claims to insurance companies, Medicare, Medicaid, or other payers, and the collection timeline depends on the payer mix, the billing infrastructure, and the complexity of the services rendered.

A practice with strong private insurance and self-pay collections might see 45-day average receivables. One heavily dependent on government payers might see 90 to 120 days. The billing and collections operation is often as important to the financial health of the practice as the clinical quality of the care.

Where cash pressure concentrates

Payer mix is the most important variable in healthcare cash flow. A practice that shifts from commercial insurance toward Medicaid, whether by choice or by patient population change, will see reimbursement rates drop and collection timelines extend simultaneously. That combination can create significant cash pressure even when patient volume is stable or growing.

Practice transitions are the second major pressure point. A physician buying an established practice is acquiring goodwill, patient relationships, and staff along with the physical assets, and all of those things can shift during transition. Patients follow doctors they trust. Staff leave when ownership changes. The acquisition that looks profitable on trailing financials can underperform during the integration period if the transition isn't managed carefully.

Structural considerations

Healthcare practice acquisitions are one of the strongest SBA use cases in small business lending. The 7(a) program handles goodwill well, which is important because in a professional practice acquisition the goodwill often represents the majority of the purchase price. The key front-end question is the same one that matters in any acquisition: what stays with the practice and what walks out the door with the seller?

Equipment financing in healthcare requires attention to useful life and technology cycle. Medical equipment that's current today may be obsolete in five years as technology advances. Financing a piece of diagnostic equipment over ten years creates a situation where the borrower is paying for obsolete equipment in years six through ten. Match amortization to the technology cycle, not just the physical life of the asset.

Watch for:

⚠️ Payer mix shifting toward government payors without corresponding revenue adjustment

⚠️ Billing days outstanding above 90, this is a collections problem, not a revenue problem

⚠️ Single-physician practice with no succession plan, the practice value disappears if the physician can't work

⚠️ Practice acquisition where the seller is the primary referral source for the patient base

⚠️ High staff turnover in clinical roles, affects patient experience and retention

⚠️ Equipment financing that extends beyond the technology refresh cycle for that specialty

Industry Four: Light Manufacturing

Long operating cycles, significant asset bases, and cash that moves slowly through the production process.

Industry Snapshot	
Cash cycle	60–180 days from raw material purchase to collection
Typical margins	Net margins 5–15% depending on product and market
Primary costs	Raw materials (30–50%), labor (20–35%), overhead and equipment
Seasonality	Varies by product; some manufacturers build inventory ahead of customer seasons
Common borrowing needs	Equipment, real estate, inventory financing, working capital, acquisition
SBA fit	Good for equipment and real estate; working capital lines typically asset-based

How money moves

Manufacturing has the longest operating cycle of any industry in this chapter. Cash goes out to buy raw materials, then sits in work-in-process inventory while the production process runs, then moves into finished goods inventory, then finally converts to a receivable when the product ships, and finally to cash when the customer pays, which might be 30 to 60 days after shipment.

This means a manufacturer can be profitable on paper and tight on cash simultaneously. A business growing at 20% annually may be consuming cash faster than it's generating it, every dollar of new revenue requires a dollar of new inventory and receivables before it becomes cash. Growth is frequently the cause of cash pressure in manufacturing, not a solution to it.

Where cash pressure concentrates

Inventory is where manufacturing cash goes to wait. Raw material prices, production efficiency, and finished goods turnover all affect how much cash is tied up in inventory at any given time. A manufacturer who holds 60 days of raw materials and 45 days of finished goods has over three months of revenue sitting in the warehouse. That's capital that isn't generating a return while it waits.

Customer concentration is the second major risk. A manufacturer with one customer representing 40% of revenue has a fragile cash flow profile regardless of how healthy the relationship appears. The loss or reduction of that customer doesn't just affect revenue, it affects the leverage the manufacturer has in managing everything else in the business.

Structural considerations

Equipment loans for manufacturers need to account for the total cost of ownership, not just the purchase price. Installation, training, tooling, and maintenance agreements can add 15 to 30% to the cost of a piece of manufacturing equipment. A loan sized to the purchase price alone leaves the borrower funding the additional costs from cash or an unprepared line draw.

Asset-based lending, where a line of credit is secured by and sized to eligible receivables and inventory, is frequently the right structure for a manufacturer with a significant balance sheet. It's more complex than a conventional revolving line but much more closely aligned to how cash actually moves through the business. Bankers working with manufacturers should understand the basics of asset-based structure even if their institution doesn't offer it, because the conversation will come up.

Watch for:

⚠️ Inventory turnover slowing year over year, often the first sign of a demand problem

⚠️ Gross margin compression without a corresponding cost explanation

⚠️ Customer concentration above 30% in a single buyer

⚠️ Equipment more than 15 years old without a replacement plan

⚠️ Working capital line fully drawn during slow production periods, may signal a permanent need

⚠️ Production capacity utilization below 60%, fixed costs are being spread too thin

Industry Five: Professional Services

Asset-light, people-heavy, and deeply dependent on the humans who deliver the work.

Industry Snapshot	
Cash cycle	30–90 days; varies by billing model and client type
Typical margins	Net margins 15–30%+ in well-run practices
Primary costs	Labor and professional staff (50–65%), occupancy, technology
Seasonality	Mild for most; accounting practices heavy in Q1, law firms vary by practice area
Common borrowing needs	Practice acquisition, partner buyout/buy-in, working capital, real estate
SBA fit	Good for acquisitions and real estate; partner transitions often conventional

How money moves

Professional services firms, accounting, law, consulting, architecture, engineering, are among the most asset-light businesses in commercial lending. They don't have inventory, their equipment needs are modest, and their collateral is primarily the relationships and expertise of their people.

Revenue is generated through time and billing. Cash comes in when clients pay invoices, which can range from immediately upon receipt to 90 days or more depending on the client type and relationship. The operating cycle is shorter than manufacturing but more variable than restaurants, and the variability often comes from client payment behavior rather than anything the firm controls.

Where cash pressure concentrates

Key-person risk is the defining structural feature of professional services lending, and it's the one most often underweighted. A three-person accounting firm where one partner holds 80% of the client relationships has a concentration risk that makes a single-customer manufacturer look diversified. If that partner leaves, retires, or becomes incapacitated, the business value can decline rapidly.

Partner transitions are the most common borrowing trigger in professional services, a retiring partner selling their equity stake to a successor, a junior partner buying into the firm, or an outside acquisition of a competing practice. These transactions require careful structuring because the asset being purchased is almost entirely goodwill, and goodwill in a professional services firm walks out the door every night.

Structural considerations

For partner buyout and buy-in transactions, the fundamental question is client retention. What percentage of the retiring partner's clients will stay with the firm? How long will the transition period be? Is the retiring partner willing to stay involved during the transition, and for how long? These aren't just due diligence questions, they're structural ones. The loan that requires 100% client retention to work is not well-structured.

Working capital lines for professional services firms often reflect billing cycle variability rather than true cash flow stress. A firm that does 40% of its annual billing in Q1 will see predictable cash pressure in Q3 even if the annual profitability is strong. Understanding whether a working capital draw reflects a business problem or a billing pattern changes both the structure and the conversation entirely.

Watch for:

⚠️ Single partner holding more than 50% of client relationships without a succession plan

⚠️ Accounts receivable aging above 90 days, collection problems in professional services often signal client dissatisfaction

⚠️ Significant decline in billable hours without a revenue explanation

⚠️ Partner departures in the 12 months preceding the loan request

⚠️ Working capital line drawn in Q2 and Q3 in a firm that should be flush from Q1 billing

⚠️ Acquisition of a retiring partner's book without a transition period agreement in place

Industry Six: Retail and Consumer-Facing Businesses

Revenue lives and dies at the register, and the balance sheet tells only half the story.

Industry Snapshot	
Cash cycle	Immediate to 30 days; most transactions settle at point of sale
Typical margins	Net margins 2–6% in physical retail; higher in specialty or service-attached concepts
Primary costs	Inventory/COGS (50–65%), labor (15–25%), occupancy (8–15%)
Seasonality	Highly variable; many retailers do 30–40% of annual revenue in Q4
Common borrowing needs	Inventory financing, equipment, leasehold improvements, owner-occupied real estate, working capital
SBA fit	Moderate, strongest for owner-occupied real estate and business acquisition; inventory lines typically conventional

How money moves

Retail businesses collect at the register, cash and card transactions settle at or near the point of sale, which means the cash conversion cycle is short by most commercial standards. The challenge isn't collecting revenue. It's managing the timing mismatch between when inventory must be purchased and when it sells.

A retailer buying seasonal merchandise in September needs to fund that inventory 60 to 90 days before the peak selling season generates cash. If the season underperforms, because of weather, competition, shifting consumer behavior, or any number of factors outside the owner's control, that inventory investment becomes a cash flow problem. The speed with which retail generates cash in good times is exactly what makes it fragile in slow ones.

Where cash pressure concentrates

Seasonality is the most defining feature of retail cash flow, and it cuts both ways. A retailer who does 35% of annual revenue in November and December builds up inventory ahead of the season, draws down the line, generates significant cash, and pays the line back in January. That's a healthy cycle. A retailer who can't pay the line back after the selling season ended has a structural problem, not a seasonal one.

Inventory management is the second major pressure point, and it's where many retail borrowers get into trouble quietly. Slow-moving or obsolete inventory doesn't disappear from the balance sheet; it just sits there, consuming capital and reducing the quality of the collateral. A retailer whose inventory turnover has been declining for two or three years is often in more distress than the income statement shows, because the margin compression from markdowns and write-offs hasn't fully worked its way through the financials yet.

Location and lease terms matter in retail the same way they matter in restaurants. A physical retailer's customer base is attached to where they are. The cost of relocating, new leasehold improvements, loss of foot traffic during transition, customer attrition, can be significant enough to threaten the business. A retailer operating on a short lease without a renewal option is carrying occupancy risk that should be visible in the structure.

Structural considerations

Working capital lines for retailers are most often inventory lines, sized to fund the purchase of merchandise ahead of the selling season and expected to pay down meaningfully after the season ends. The key front-end question is whether the line actually does pay down, and when. A line that never clears or that only partially pays back after peak season is signaling that the retailer is funding something beyond seasonal inventory, and that something needs to be identified before the next renewal.

Owner-occupied real estate is a strong fit for established retailers in stable locations. The same logic that applies to restaurants applies here: converting rent to debt service stabilizes the occupancy cost and eliminates the relocation risk of a landlord-controlled lease. The SBA 504 program is often the right tool, particularly for retailers who have strong cash flow but limited down payment liquidity after years of funding growth from retained earnings.

Leasehold improvements deserve specific attention. A retailer who spends $150,000 building out a leased space has created a real asset that has zero value outside that location. If the lease ends, or if the business closes, those improvements are gone. Financing leasehold improvements requires an honest view of the lease term, the renewal probability, and whether the business generates enough return from that space to justify the investment.

Watch for:

⚠️ Line of credit that doesn't pay down after the seasonal selling period, permanent need disguised as working capital

⚠️ Inventory turnover declining year over year without a merchandising explanation

⚠️ Gross margin compression alongside flat or growing revenue, often signals markdowns or theft

⚠️ Lease with fewer than 3 years remaining in a location-dependent business

⚠️ Heavy revenue concentration in one season without adequate reserves to fund the off-season

⚠️ Significant leasehold improvement investment with a short or uncertain lease term

⚠️ Owner compensation declining while revenue holds, may signal the owner is managing cash by deferring their own draw

Building Your Own Pattern Recognition

Six industries. The same thinking process in each one.

When you encounter an industry you haven't seen before, and you will, because the business world is far more varied than any chapter can cover, here's how to start building the pattern quickly.

Step one: Ask the four core questions first

Before you do any research, before you talk to anyone else, apply the four questions from the beginning of this chapter: how does money come in, when does cash go out, what creates pressure, and what does stress look like? You'll get partial answers from the borrower's own explanation of their business. Fill in the gaps from everything else.

Step two: Find a comparable business you understand

Every unfamiliar industry has structural similarities to something you've already seen. A veterinary practice has a lot in common with a medical practice. A specialty food manufacturer has a lot in common with a general manufacturer. A staffing agency has a lot in common with a contractor. Identify the closest parallel and ask: where does this business differ from the one I know? The differences are where the new pattern lives.

Step three: Talk to the borrower about the industry, not just the business

One of the most useful questions a banker can ask a business owner is: "What do you wish bankers understood about your industry that they usually don't?" The answers are almost always genuinely useful, and they signal to the borrower that you're interested in their world, not just their financial statements.

Step four: Look at the trailing financials for the pattern, not just the numbers

Once you have a mental model of how the industry should work, look at the financials to see if the business matches the model. Does the receivables balance grow in the right months and shrink in the right months? Does the inventory level reflect the production cycle you'd expect? Does the cash balance dip when you'd expect it to and recover when you'd expect it to? The financials of a healthy business in a given industry tend to follow a pattern. Deviation from the pattern is worth understanding.

Step five: Find one experienced lender in that industry and ask them one question

Every commercial lending team has someone who's done a lot of deals in a specific industry. Find them. Ask: "What's the thing that always surprises newer bankers about lending to this type of business?" That answer, in one minute, is often worth more than an hour of independent research.

> ***Pattern recognition isn't memorized. It's built, one business, one conversation, one deal at a time. The banker who approaches every new industry with genuine curiosity develops it faster than the one who waits to feel ready.***

What This Chapter Is Really About

The six industries covered here are not a comprehensive guide to any of them. They're demonstrations of a consistent way of thinking, one that starts with cash flow, moves through structure, and ends with the specific warning signs that experience produces and textbooks rarely capture.

The banker who has read this chapter hasn't become an expert in restaurants or retail. They've built a process for developing expertise in whatever industry is sitting across from them next.

That process, the four questions, the comparable business, the borrower's own knowledge, the pattern in the financials, and the experienced colleague, is what turns a generalist commercial banker into one who borrowers in every industry feel genuinely understood by.

> ***Industry knowledge isn't a prerequisite for good commercial lending. Curiosity is. The rest follows.***

In the next chapter, we'll close the front-end framework with the mindset that ties everything together, the way of thinking that a banker carries into every commercial conversation, regardless of industry, deal size, or how many times they've seen the pattern before.

CHAPTER 20

The Front-End Lending Mindset

Commercial lending doesn't succeed because bankers know more formulas.

It succeeds because they think differently.

By now, you've seen that front-end lending isn't about products, policies, or approval mechanics. It's about how you *see* a business, how you *frame* risk, and how you *shape* structure long before underwriting ever gets involved.

This final chapter doesn't introduce new concepts. It pulls together everything you've read, not as a checklist, but as a way of thinking you can carry into every commercial conversation from here.

The Quiet Truth About Good Loans

Most good commercial loans share three things: they are understandable, they are intentional, and they age well.

They don't rely on perfect execution. They don't require heroic assumptions. They don't surprise anyone six months later. When a loan lands on someone's desk a year after closing and nothing feels off, that's not luck.

> ***That's front-end discipline. Quiet, unannounced, and exactly what it's supposed to be.***

What Bankers Really Do

Bankers are not gatekeepers. They are not salespeople. They are not junior underwriters.

They are **risk translators**.

They take business reality, borrower behavior, cash flow dynamics, and uncertainty, and translate all of it into structure the bank can live with.

That translation happens before credit memos, before loan committees, before legal documents.

> ***When the translation is done well at the front end, everything downstream becomes easier. When it's skipped, everything downstream becomes harder.***

That's the simplest summary of what this book has been about.

The Five Questions That Never Fail

Everything in this book can be reduced to five questions. Before any deal moves forward, a banker should be able to answer all five clearly, honestly, and in plain language.

If the answers are fuzzy, the deal isn't ready.

1. **What is really happening inside this business?** Not the pitch, the operating reality.
2. **Why does this business need debt right now?** Timing matters as much as purpose.
3. **How will this loan be repaid under normal conditions?** Not best-case conditions.
4. **What happens if things don't go as planned?** Structure exists for this moment.
5. **Does this loan still make sense six months from now?** Good loans age quietly.

If you can answer those five questions honestly, structure becomes obvious. If you can't, there's more work to do, and doing it now is far better than doing it later.

When the Right Answer Is "Not Yet"

One of the hardest lessons in front-end lending is this: not every good business is ready for a good loan.

Timing matters. Structure matters. Discipline matters. And sometimes the most responsible thing a banker can do is slow things down, tell a borrower what would need to change, and agree to revisit when the conditions are right.

Saying "not yet" preserves trust, prevents regret, and often leads to better deals later, deals built on a stronger foundation, with a borrower who respects the banker more, not less, for being direct.

> ***Waiting is a form of structure. Bankers who understand this don't feel pressure to force outcomes that aren't ready.***

What This Book Is, and Isn't

This book was never about teaching you to underwrite, memorize ratios, navigate policy manuals, or win arguments with credit.

It's about the part of commercial lending most people never get formally taught: seeing risk earlier, asking better questions, structuring more thoughtfully, and preventing problems before they exist.

That front-end work is where outcomes are actually decided. By the time a deal reaches underwriting, most of the result is already determined. The banker who shapes the deal before it gets there, who asks the hard question, resizes the amount, separates the needs, pushes back on the timeline, that banker is doing the most important work in the process.

Why Front-End Discipline Builds Trust

Trust in commercial lending doesn't come from approval rates. It comes from predictable judgment.

Borrowers trust bankers who explain structure clearly, don't oversell flexibility, set expectations early, and stay consistent when circumstances change. Credit trusts bankers who surface risk honestly, fix structure before it becomes a problem, and deliver clean, thoughtful deals that don't require advocacy to get through.

Both kinds of trust are built the same way: by doing the front-end work with discipline and care, every time, regardless of the size of the deal or the familiarity of the relationship.

The Banker You Are Becoming

If this book has done its job, you no longer see commercial lending as a set of products, a black box called "credit," or a yes-or-no decision that happens somewhere above you.

You see it as a conversation, and a diagnostic process, and a craft.

You understand that your real influence happens *before* the loan exists. That the questions you ask in the first conversation shape everything that follows. That structure is not something credit invents, it's something you bring to them, already thought through, already tested, already honest about its own limitations.

> ***That's where good lending lives. And now you know how to work there.***

One Final Discipline to Carry Forward

As you move into more commercial conversations, with borrowers, with credit, with colleagues who are still figuring this out, carry one question with you:

> ***If this loan becomes a problem, will I be surprised?***

If the answer is yes, slow down. There's something you haven't resolved yet.

If the answer is no, structure is probably doing its job.

Good lending doesn't eliminate risk. It eliminates surprise. And the front end, the conversation, the discovery, the framing, the structuring, the pressure-testing, is where that work happens.

Closing Thought

Commercial lending is not about being aggressive or conservative.

It's about being **intentional**.

When bankers think clearly, structure thoughtfully, and communicate honestly, loans don't just get approved, they perform. Quietly. Predictably. Over time. Without drama, without surprises, without the slow accumulation of regret that comes from a loan that should have been shaped differently at the start.

That's the goal.

And now, you know how to build it.

Deal Clinic 1 - The Line That Never Pays Down

Pattern: "We just need a line of credit."

Business: A residential painting contractor, eight years in business, $1.2M annual revenue, three full-time employees plus seasonal labor.

Version A: What Went Wrong	Version B: What Good Structure Looks Like
$250,000 revolving line, no clean-up requirement, annual renewal	$120,000 revolving line with 30-day annual clean-up + $85,000 equipment term loan

VERSION A: WHAT WENT WRONG

The banker met the owner, Tony, in March. Tony explained that his business was growing and he needed flexibility. The banker asked how much he was thinking. Tony said $250,000. The banker ran the numbers, confirmed the business qualified, and submitted the request.

What the banker didn't ask: what specifically was the line for? How did cash move through the business? When did Tony expect to pay it down?

What the banker didn't notice: Tony's previous line at another bank had been fully drawn for eleven months before he moved his relationship. The deposit history showed consistent cash inflows but also consistent large transfers out, pattern consistent with a business running tight on operating cash.

The line was approved. By August it was fully drawn. By the following March it was still fully drawn. At renewal the banker recommended approval again. "It's stable," the memo said. "No issues."

Two years later Tony's largest customer, a property management company representing 38% of his revenue, moved to a competitor.

Revenue dropped 30% in 90 days. The line was fully drawn. Tony had no operating reserve. The bank had no early warning. The loan became a problem.

> **What went wrong:** The banker treated the line as a qualification exercise rather than a structural question. Discovery never happened. The permanently drawn balance, visible from day one in the deposit history, was never flagged. The concentration risk in a single customer was never surfaced. "Stable" and "healthy" are not the same thing.

VERSION B: WHAT GOOD STRUCTURE LOOKS LIKE

A different banker met Tony and asked the same opening question she asked every contractor: "Walk me through a typical job, from when you quote it to when you get paid."

Tony explained: he quotes, wins the job, buys materials upfront ($8,000–$15,000 per job), pays crew weekly, and collects 30–60 days after completion. He has eight to twelve jobs running simultaneously in peak season.

The banker did the math. Peak exposure, materials and labor out before collections in, was about $110,000 in a busy month. She also noticed that Tony had two pieces of aging equipment: a sprayer system and a cargo van, both over seven years old.

She came back with a different structure than Tony asked for.

"You don't need $250,000," she said. "Your peak cash gap is about $110,000. I'd rather build you a $120,000 line that you actually use fully and pay down every winter, that's a line that renews easily because the story makes sense. The equipment is a separate need. Let's finance that with a five-year term loan so you're not funding long-life assets on a revolving line."

She also asked about customers. When Tony mentioned one property manager represented about 40% of his revenue, she flagged it directly. "That's something we'll note in the structure. It's not a problem right now, but it's something to watch. If that relationship ever shifted, I'd want to know early."

The line had a 30-day annual clean-up requirement. It paid to zero every January when Tony's work slowed. At renewal each year, the pattern was clean. Three years later, when Tony lost the property management customer, he had $74,000 available on his line and six weeks of operating reserves. He called his banker before it became a crisis. They restructured proactively.

> **How good structure fixes it:** Discovery surfaced the real cash gap, the equipment need, and the concentration risk before the loan was built. Right-sizing the line to the actual pattern made it a story credit could read clearly. The clean-up requirement created an annual signal. The concentration conversation built trust and established early-warning behavior that paid off when it mattered.

> **The lesson:** *A line that never pays down isn't a line, it's term debt with no discipline. The banker who asks 'when does this pay to zero?' before closing the loan is the banker who never has to ask 'why is this still fully drawn?' at renewal.*

Deal Clinic 2 - The Growth Loan That Arrived Too Early

Pattern: "This loan will let us grow."

Business: A boutique fitness studio, four years in business, $680,000 annual revenue, one location, profitable for the past two years.

Version A: What Went Wrong	Version B: What Good Structure Looks Like
$420,000 term loan for second location build-out, approved on projected revenue	$180,000 equipment/build-out loan for first location expansion + phased second location commitment

VERSION A: WHAT WENT WRONG

The owner, Priya, had a compelling story. One successful location, strong member retention, a waiting list for classes. She'd found a second space two miles away and had a letter of intent signed. Her banker was excited.

The loan was sized on projected revenue from the second location: $340,000 in year one, growing to $520,000 by year three. The build-out was $380,000 and Priya wanted $40,000 for working capital during the ramp. The banker submitted it as a $420,000 term loan on a seven-year amortization.

What the projections assumed: the second location would reach break-even in month seven. Priya had never opened a second location before. The projections were built from the first location's performance metrics, reasonable in concept, but the first location had taken fourteen months to reach break-even.

The loan closed in April. The second location opened in September, later than planned due to permitting delays. By the following April, it was at 60% of projected membership. Cash flow from location two was not covering its debt service. Priya was covering the gap from location one's cash flow. Location one began to show strain by summer.

> **What went wrong:** The banker approved a growth loan on projections that had never been stress-tested against the first location's actual ramp timeline. The working capital cushion was too thin for a business opening its first second location. There was no phasing, no review trigger, and no conversation about what 'month seven break-even' actually required to happen.

VERSION B: WHAT GOOD STRUCTURE LOOKS LIKE

A different banker asked Priya a question that changed the whole conversation: "How long did it take your first location to break even?"

Fourteen months, Priya said.

The banker ran the second location projections against a fourteen-month ramp rather than seven. The picture changed significantly. Under a fourteen-month ramp, Priya would need approximately $95,000 in operating support during the ramp period, nearly double the $40,000 she'd requested for working capital.

The banker also looked at location one's cash flow under the scenario where it had to fund the gap. It could, but barely. There was no margin for error at the original location if something went wrong.

She came back to Priya with a different approach. "I think the second location is the right move. I don't think it's the right move right now, and here's what I mean."

Instead of a second location build-out loan, she proposed: a $180,000 equipment and improvement loan for location one, new equipment, expanded changing rooms, and two additional class formats that the current space could support. This would increase location one's revenue ceiling and build a larger cash reserve over the next 18 months. Then, with a stronger base and more cash, the second location conversation would be better supported.

Priya pushed back initially. The second space wouldn't be available forever. The banker acknowledged that directly: "If this specific space is the right one and you want to move forward now, we can do that. But I want you to know what the structure requires and what happens if the ramp takes as long as your first location did. If you still want to proceed after seeing that, I'll build the best loan I can."

Priya chose to wait. Eighteen months later she opened the second location with a stronger cash position, a larger member base at location one to cross-promote, and a realistic model built on fourteen months of ramp, not seven. It broke even in month eleven.

> **How good structure fixes it:** Asking about the first location's actual ramp timeline, one question, changed the entire structural picture. The banker didn't decline the deal. She gave Priya the real information and let her decide. Phasing the financing around location one's capacity to grow first produced a second location that opened from strength rather than hope.

> **The lesson:** *Growth loans should be sized to carry the business through a realistic ramp, not an optimistic one. The most useful question a banker can ask before any expansion loan is: 'What did the last expansion actually take, in time, in cash, in management attention?'*

Deal Clinic 3 - The Refinance That Didn't Fix Anything

Pattern: "We want to refinance existing debt."

Business: An independent auto repair shop, twelve years in business, $1.8M annual revenue, owner-operated with six technicians.

Version A: What Went Wrong	Version B: What Good Structure Looks Like
$310,000 consolidation loan rolling four obligations into one, lower payment, longer term	Selective refinancing of two obligations + 90-day hold on the rest pending cash flow review

VERSION A: WHAT WENT WRONG

Marcus came in looking to simplify. He had four obligations: a $95,000 equipment loan at a community bank, a $74,000 balance on a line of credit at another institution, an $88,000 SBA loan from six years ago, and a $53,000 personal loan he'd taken to cover a cash shortfall two years earlier.

His pitch was reasonable: one payment, lower monthly outgo, easier to manage. The banker ran the numbers. A $310,000 consolidation loan at 8.5% over ten years produced a monthly payment of $3,840, lower than the combined payments by about $1,100.

What the banker didn't ask: why were there four separate obligations in the first place? Why had Marcus needed a personal loan to cover a cash shortfall two years ago? Why was a revolving line carrying a $74,000 balance that didn't appear to be moving?

The consolidation closed. Marcus's cash flow improved immediately, by $1,100 a month. Twelve months later the line of credit was back to $74,000. He'd started using it again after paying it off at close. The personal loan savings had gone back into operations rather than reserves. The underlying cash flow issue, a business that spent as much as it earned, hadn't changed. It just had more runway.

> **What went wrong:** The banker solved the symptom, payment complexity, without diagnosing the cause. The personal loan was a major signal: a business owner borrowing personally to fund operations is a business with a structural cash flow problem, not a payment management problem. The consolidation gave Marcus room to breathe and nothing to change.

VERSION B: WHAT GOOD STRUCTURE LOOKS LIKE

A different banker looked at the same four obligations and asked one question before touching the structure: "Tell me about the personal loan. What happened two years ago?"

Marcus explained: a key technician had left unexpectedly, taking two major fleet accounts with him. Revenue had dropped $22,000 a month for about five months before Marcus rebuilt the book. He'd used the personal loan to bridge the gap rather than miss payroll.

The banker noted two things. First, the revenue had recovered, the business was genuinely strong. Second, the line of credit hadn't been paid down during the recovery, which meant the cash that came back in had gone somewhere else: presumably into operations and owner draws.

She proposed a different structure. The equipment loan and the SBA loan had logical underlying purposes and appropriate terms, she recommended leaving those in place. The personal loan had a high rate and no business purpose going forward, she recommended refinancing that into a clean five-year term loan. The line of credit she recommended restructuring with a 60-day paydown requirement before renewal and a covenant that it could not be drawn above $40,000 without prior discussion.

She was direct with Marcus: "The consolidation you're asking for will lower your payment and give you more cash each month. That's true. But based on what I'm seeing, more cash hasn't historically stayed in the business, it's gone out. I'd rather build something that forces a little discipline into the structure than give you a lower payment that creates the same situation in 18 months."

Marcus pushed back. The banker held it. The restructure went forward on her terms. At the 18-month mark, the line was at $31,000, the first time it had been below $60,000 in four years. Marcus called to say the discipline had been annoying and useful in equal measure.

> **How good structure fixes it:** Asking about the personal loan surfaced the real story: a cash flow pattern that spent what it earned. Selective refinancing, fixing what needed fixing, leaving what was working, adding discipline to what was drifting, produced a structure that improved the business rather than just rearranging its obligations.

> **The lesson:** *Refinancing should improve alignment, not just reduce payments. Before consolidating anything, ask: why do these obligations exist, and what changes this time? If the answer is 'nothing changes,' the refinance is a postponement.*

Deal Clinic 4 - The Acquisition That Forgot About Integration

Pattern: "We're buying something."

Business: A regional staffing agency, nine years in business, $3.4M annual revenue, acquiring a smaller competitor at $890,000.

Version A: What Went Wrong	Version B: What Good Structure Looks Like
$801,000 SBA 7(a) acquisition loan (10% down), no working capital reserve, full integration assumed at close	$756,000 acquisition loan (15% down) + $85,000 working capital line + 12-month integration review covenant

VERSION A: WHAT WENT WRONG

The buyer, Diane, had built her staffing agency methodically over nine years. She ran a tight operation. The acquisition target, a smaller agency with $1.1M in revenue, had three large clients that Diane wanted. The seller was retiring. The price was fair.

The banker ran the combined entity financials. Adding the target's historical revenue to Diane's operation showed a strong combined business. DSCR on the acquisition loan looked comfortable. The loan went through SBA at 10% down.

What no one modeled: the target's three large clients had relationships with the seller personally, not with the agency. Two of them had never met Diane. The seller had agreed to a 60-day transition period. The banker never asked what happened after day 61.

Post-close, one large client moved to another agency within 90 days, citing a preference for their existing relationship. A second reduced their volume by half while they "evaluated options." Combined revenue in the first year post-acquisition was $3.8M, versus the $4.5M the combined projections had shown. Debt service coverage dropped below 1.0x by month ten.

> **What went wrong:** The acquisition was underwritten on combined historical revenues that included the seller's personal relationships. No one asked: what happens if the clients follow the seller? No working capital buffer existed for the transition period. The 60-day seller involvement was insufficient for a business built on personal relationships.

VERSION B: WHAT GOOD STRUCTURE LOOKS LIKE

A different banker asked Diane one question that reframed the entire deal: "These three clients, do they have a relationship with the agency or with the owner?"

Diane paused. Mostly with the owner, she admitted. She knew them through him.

The banker ran two scenarios: one where all three clients stayed, one where one left and one reduced volume, which she described as a conservative but realistic transition scenario for a relationship-based business. Under the conservative scenario, first-year revenue was closer to $3.9M than $4.5M. DSCR was tighter but workable, if the structure had a buffer.

She restructured the approach in three ways. First, she increased the down payment from 10% to 15%, reducing the loan to $756,000 and improving the debt service picture under the conservative scenario. Second, she added an $85,000 working capital line, not to be drawn at close, but available during the integration period if client revenue came in slower than projected. Third, she built a 12-month review into the loan covenants, requiring updated financials and a brief relationship retention report at month six and month twelve.

She also asked Diane to negotiate a longer seller involvement period, six months instead of two, with the seller making client introductions and co-attending relationship meetings during the transition. Diane went back to the seller. He agreed to four months.

The acquisition closed. One client reduced volume in month three, as anticipated. The working capital line was drawn $40,000 at peak. By month eight it was repaid. The other two clients stayed and grew with Diane over the following two years.

> **How good structure fixes it:** One question about relationship vs. institutional client loyalty changed the entire risk picture. Increasing down payment, adding a working capital buffer, extending seller involvement, and building in a structured review turned a structurally fragile acquisition into one that could absorb the client attrition that was always the most likely risk.

> **The lesson:** *Acquisitions are underwritten on combined historical numbers. They perform on post-close dynamics. The front-end question that matters most is not 'what did this business earn?', it's 'what walks out the door when the seller does?'*

Deal Clinic 5 - The Relationship Deal That Should Have Been Harder

Pattern: "This is a relationship deal."

Business: A specialty printing company, sixteen years in business, $2.2M annual revenue, long-standing bank relationship.

Version A: What Went Wrong	Version B: What Good Structure Looks Like
$480,000 term loan approved on relationship history; weakening financials acknowledged but not acted on	$280,000 right-sized term loan with tighter covenants, 18-month review trigger, and direct conversation about declining margins

VERSION A: WHAT WENT WRONG

Frank had been a customer for eleven years. He'd borrowed twice before, both times without incident. He was well-liked, prompt with information, and reasonable to work with. His banker had been calling on him for seven of those years.

Frank came in for a $480,000 equipment loan, new digital printing presses to replace aging equipment and expand into large-format work. The banker pulled the financials. Revenue was flat for three years. Margins had compressed from 18% to 11%. The explanation, pricing pressure, digital competition, a few customers moving in-house, sounded reasonable. Frank was confident the new equipment would help him compete.

The banker wrote it up. In the credit memo he noted the margin compression and characterized it as "industry-wide" and "temporary." He described Frank as "a proven borrower with an excellent track record." The loan was approved.

Eighteen months later Frank's largest customer, responsible for 29% of revenue, moved its printing in-house using equipment Frank had helped them spec out. Revenue dropped $420,000. The new presses, still on the books, were now producing output for a customer base that had shrunk faster than the equipment could generate volume to support the loan.

> **What went wrong:** The relationship created permission to overlook what the financials were clearly showing. Three years of flat revenue and seven points of margin compression is not a temporary industry condition, it's a trend. The credit memo used the relationship as a substitute for structural analysis. Frank's track record was real. The forward-looking risk was also real, and it wasn't named.

VERSION B: WHAT GOOD STRUCTURE LOOKS LIKE

A different banker, newer to the relationship, covering while Frank's primary banker was on leave, pulled the last three years of financials before the first meeting. She saw the same numbers.

In the meeting she was direct but careful. "I want to be upfront with you. I've looked at three years of financials and I see something I want to understand before we talk about the equipment. Revenue is flat and margins have come down about seven points. Walk me through what's driving that."

Frank gave the same explanation: pricing pressure, digital competition. She asked a follow-up: "What's the plan for the new equipment specifically, which customers or segments does it let you go after that you can't serve today?"

Frank's answer was general. He talked about large-format printing as a growth market. He mentioned a few prospects but no signed work. He referenced his largest customer as likely to expand volume once he had the new capability.

She made two decisions. First, she right-sized the loan. Frank had asked for $480,000 for two presses. She recommended one press at $280,000, the one with the clearest near-term revenue application, and suggested revisiting the second if the large-format revenue materialized within 18 months.

Second, she built a covenant into the loan: if EBITDA declined more than 15% from the trailing twelve months at any annual review, it triggered a structured conversation, not a default, but a mandatory check-in before the situation deteriorated further.

Third, she had the customer concentration conversation directly. "Your largest customer is 29% of revenue. I'm not saying they're going anywhere, but it's a number worth naming. If that relationship ever changed, I'd want to know early enough to be helpful."

Frank was a little surprised by the conversation. He'd expected the usual process. He said later it was the most useful loan conversation he'd had in years.

The second press was never needed, Frank's largest customer moved in-house 14 months after close. But with a $280,000 loan instead of $480,000, and with the EBITDA covenant triggering a structured conversation at the 12-month review, the bank had time to work with Frank on a path forward before the situation became a crisis.

How good structure fixes it: Right-sizing the loan based on demonstrable near-term revenue application, not aspiration. Building a structured early-warning covenant rather than hoping history would hold. Having the customer concentration conversation before it became relevant. Three front-end decisions that converted a relationship deal into a well-structured one.

The lesson: *Strong relationships deserve strong structure, not less of it. A banker who lets history substitute for analysis is not protecting a relationship. They're deferring the harder conversation to the worst possible moment. Frank deserved honesty earlier. The bank did too.*

What the Clinic Is Really Showing

Five patterns. Ten versions. Every Version B follows the same logic:

- Discovery came before structure
- The real problem was named, not assumed
- The loan was sized to the actual need, not the ask
- Risk was identified and either addressed structurally or named explicitly
- The borrower left the conversation with more clarity than they arrived with

None of the Version B bankers had better borrowers. They had better questions.

> ***Pattern recognition speeds up judgment. The banker who has seen the line that never pays down before will ask the clean-up question automatically. The one who hasn't will find out at renewal. This is how experience becomes structure, and structure becomes outcomes.***

Appendix B: The Conversation Guide

This book has covered what to think. This chapter is about what to say.

Most commercial lending conversations don't fail because the banker didn't understand the structure. They fail because the banker didn't know how to say something difficult in a way the borrower could hear, or they softened something that needed to stay firm, or they explained a term defensively and created resistance that didn't need to exist.

This guide covers eight of the most common and most challenging front-end conversation moments. Each one includes the context, what most bankers get wrong, a fully worked example, and the principle underneath it.

A note on the dialogue: real conversations are messier than any example can capture. Borrowers interrupt, change direction, and sometimes say things that don't fit the expected path. The exchanges here are realistic, not sanitized, but they're still cleaner than what you'll encounter. Treat them as demonstrations of the approach, not scripts to follow word for word.

> ***These are not scripts. They are frameworks. The words you use should sound like you. The approach should stay consistent.***

Blue text marks the banker throughout all dialogue examples.

Conversation One: Opening a Discovery Call

A borrower has reached out about a loan. You've had a brief initial call. Now you're sitting down, in person or by phone, for the real conversation. You need to understand the business before you can say anything useful about the loan.

What most bankers do wrong

They start with the financial checklist. Tax returns, financial statements, ownership structure, time in business. All of that matters eventually, but leading with it signals that you're processing the borrower, not listening to them. The most important information in a discovery call, the owner's real motivation, the timing pressure, the thing they're worried about but haven't said yet, almost never surfaces in response to a direct question. It surfaces when someone feels understood enough to offer it.

The other trap is anchoring on the loan request too early. A borrower who says they need a $400,000 line of credit may be right, or may be describing their version of a solution to a problem they haven't fully diagnosed. Discovery is the diagnostic step. You can't skip it and structure well.

How it sounds

The business: a landscaping company, seven years in operation, $1.4M in revenue. The owner has called about a line of credit. This is the follow-up conversation.

> **Banker:** "Before we get into numbers, help me understand the business. Walk me through how a typical week runs, how money comes in, where it goes, what keeps you up at night."
>
> **Owner:** "Sure. We do mostly commercial contracts, landscape maintenance for office parks and HOAs. Those pay monthly. But we're paying our crews weekly and buying materials before every job starts."
>
> **Banker:** "So your cash goes out before it comes back in. How long is that gap, typically?"
>
> **Owner:** "Three to five weeks on most jobs. Sometimes longer if the client is slow on invoices."
>
> **Banker:** "And what's been covering that gap up until now?"
>
> **Owner:** "Mostly our own reserves. But we've been growing fast and the reserves just aren't keeping up. Last spring we had to delay a payroll by three days and it was not a good week."

Banker: "That's useful. Delayed payroll usually means you're at peak borrowing need and the reserves aren't quite sized to the volume. Has the business added any new large contracts in the last year?"

Owner: "Two. One started in March, one in July. They're our two biggest clients now."

Banker: "Do you know what percentage of your revenue those two represent together?"

Owner: "Probably 45, maybe 50 percent combined."

Banker: "Okay. I want to make a note of that for later, that level of concentration in two clients is something we'll want to think about structurally. Not a problem right now, but worth naming. What else is on your mind about the business that you haven't said yet?"

Owner: "Honestly? I'm worried about what happens if I lose one of those contracts. The line was my wife's idea. She thinks we need the cushion. I think we need to just grow more."

Banker: "That's a genuinely important tension, and I'm glad you said it. Because the right structure for 'we need a cushion' looks different from the right structure for 'we need capital to grow.' Let's figure out which one this actually is before we talk about how much."

> **What happened here:** The banker heard four things the borrower didn't lead with: a payroll near-miss that reveals how thin the reserve is, two clients representing nearly half of revenue (concentration risk), a gap between the owner's motivation and the spouse's motivation, and the real question underneath the request: cushion vs. growth capital. None of that came from asking about tax returns.

The principle

Discovery is not data collection. It's model-building. By the time you've finished a good discovery conversation, you should be able to close your notebook and describe how cash moves through the business, where the pressure concentrates, what the owner's real concern is, and roughly what kind of structure the deal needs. If you can't do that, discovery isn't done.

The question "what else is on your mind that you haven't said yet?" is one of the most reliably useful questions in a discovery call. Ask it once, toward the end. Then be quiet.

Conversation Two: Reframing What the Borrower Actually Needs

A borrower has asked for a specific loan type or amount. Discovery has revealed that their request doesn't quite match the real problem. You need to redirect without making them feel corrected, and you need to hold the reframe when they push back.

What most bankers do wrong

There are two failure modes. The first is capitulation: accepting the borrower's request at face value and building toward the wrong structure, which produces a loan that either gets declined or creates problems later. The second is confrontation: telling the borrower they're wrong in a way that puts them on the defensive and makes the banker the obstacle.

The harder version of this conversation is when the borrower doesn't accept the reframe immediately. Many guides show the borrower saying "I never thought about it that way" and moving on. Real borrowers often push back. They have a reason they asked for what they asked for, and they don't always find the banker's reframe immediately convincing. Being prepared for that friction is part of doing this well.

How it sounds

Same landscaping business. The owner has come in asking for a $350,000 line of credit.

> **Owner:** "We need a $350,000 line. We need the flexibility."

Banker: "Tell me more about flexibility, what specifically are you trying to be able to do that you can't do right now?"

Owner: "We have a big equipment purchase coming. One of our mowers is done, and we need a new truck. That's probably $130,000 combined. And then we need the working capital cushion for the busy season."

Banker: "So there are two different things here. One is equipment that's going to be useful for the next six or seven years. The other is seasonal cash flow that'll repeat every year. Those are structurally different needs, and trying to solve both with one line of credit usually makes both harder to manage. Can I show you what I mean?"

Owner: "I've always just used a line for everything. It's simpler."

Banker: "I understand why it feels that way. But here's what actually happens. If we put the equipment on the line, that $130,000 is sitting there permanently, because equipment doesn't pay itself off through your operating cycle. It just stays drawn. Now your working capital line is $130,000 smaller than you thought, and during peak season when you actually need it, you don't have it."

Owner: "Okay, I see that. But why can't I just have a bigger line to cover both?"

Banker: "You could. But a $350,000 line where $130,000 is permanently committed to equipment isn't really a $350,000 line, it's a $220,000 line with $130,000 in disguise. And lines that are permanently partially drawn are harder to renew, because the bank has to keep explaining why $130,000 never moves. A term loan for the equipment and a working capital line sized to your actual seasonal need is two smaller, cleaner facilities that are each easier to manage and each easier to renew. The total is probably similar. The structure is much clearer."

Owner: "What does that look like in terms of payments?"

Banker: "Let's work through it. The $130,000 equipment piece on a five-year term is roughly $2,600 a month. The working capital line, let's talk about what you actually need seasonally, I'd rather size that to your peak cash gap than to a round number. What's your biggest month for cash outflows?"

> **What happened here:** The borrower pushed back twice, first defending simplicity, then asking for a bigger line anyway. The banker didn't back down or apologize. They named the specific mechanism by which the 'simple' approach creates complexity later. By the end of the exchange the borrower is asking about payments on the right structure, not defending the wrong one.

The principle

Reframing is translation, not correction. But translation sometimes requires more than one attempt. When a borrower pushes back on a reframe, the right response is not to cave and not to repeat yourself louder, it's to name the specific mechanism by which the original request creates a problem. Abstract structural arguments don't land. Concrete consequences do.

Conversation Three: Explaining a Structure Change the Borrower Didn't Ask For

You've shaped the structure and it looks different from what the borrower originally requested, smaller amount, different product type, shorter term. You need to explain why without it feeling like a downgrade, and you need to hold it when the borrower expresses disappointment.

What most bankers do wrong

Three common failures: explaining defensively ("credit requires this"), apologetically ("I wish I could do more"), or technically ("the DSCR doesn't support the full amount"). Each creates a different problem. Defensive explanations make the bank sound bureaucratic. Apologetic ones signal the banker doesn't believe in the structure. Technical ones leave the borrower confused and, often, more suspicious.

The deeper mistake is framing the change as a limitation rather than a design decision. A smaller loan isn't always a lesser outcome, it's sometimes a better one. The banker who can make that case honestly and specifically builds more trust than the one who delivers good news poorly.

How it sounds

A retail bakery owner came in for a $300,000 line of credit. After discovery and financial review, the banker is recommending a $165,000 line.

> **Banker:** "I want to walk you through what I'm recommending, because it's different from what you came in asking for. I'd rather explain it now than have you hear a different number and wonder why."
>
> **Owner:** "Okay."
>
> **Banker:** "You asked for $300,000. I'm recommending $165,000. Here's why. Your peak borrowing need, based on the last two full years of deposit history, is about $145,000. That's your worst month, October, when you're building inventory for the holiday season and payroll is highest. A $165,000 line covers that with some room. A $300,000 line gives you $135,000 you'll never use."
>
> **Owner:** "I wanted the extra cushion in case things change."
>
> **Banker:** "I understand that instinct. But here's the thing about unused credit on a line: it doesn't help you at renewal if the bank is looking at a line that's never been more than 55% utilized. It actually makes the renewal harder, because the question becomes 'why do they need $300,000 when they've never used more than $165,000?' A line sized to your actual peak is easier to renew every year. And if your business grows and the need genuinely changes, we can revisit the limit."
>
> **Owner:** "What if I have an emergency and the line isn't big enough?"
>
> **Banker:** "That's the right question to ask. What kind of emergency are you thinking about?"

Owner: "Like if an oven breaks down. Or I need to hire people fast."

Banker: "An oven is equipment, that's a different instrument than a working capital line. If an oven breaks down, we'd finance it as a term loan, not a line draw. For hiring, I'd want to understand the timing better, but a $165,000 line that's currently at zero is $165,000 of available emergency capacity. That's not nothing."

Owner: "I guess I just always thought more was better."

Banker: "A lot of borrowers do. In this case, I think right-sized is better. A line you fully use and pay down is a stronger story than a line you partially use. And it's a better picture of your business."

> **What happened here:** The borrower raised a real concern about cushion and emergencies. The banker didn't dismiss it, they asked what kind of emergency and showed that the two scenarios the borrower named (equipment failure, hiring) were either handled by a different instrument or covered by the recommended limit. By the end the banker has held the number and explained it in terms of the borrower's own business history and future conversations.

> **Watch out:** Don't cave on amount just because a borrower says they wanted more. If the analysis supports $165,000 and not $300,000, that's the recommendation. "I'll see what I can do" is not a structural answer.

The principle

Explain structure in terms of the borrower's own business history and future conversations, not the bank's requirements. When a borrower understands why a structure fits their specific situation, they stop comparing it to what they originally asked for and start evaluating it on its own merits. Hold the position. Explain it repeatedly if necessary. The borrower's comfort with the number usually follows their understanding of why it's right.

Conversation Four: Pushing Back on an Oversized Request

A borrower is asking for significantly more than the structure supports, they've added a buffer or a wish list to a real need. You need to get to the right number without making the borrower feel accused of asking for too much.

What most bankers do wrong

Two failure modes again. The first is going along with the number to avoid conflict, then letting credit decline it or coming back later with a lower number, which makes the banker look weak and leaves the borrower confused about what changed. The second is refusing the number flatly without decomposing it, which makes the banker look rigid and leaves the borrower without a path forward.

The most effective approach doesn't involve the banker announcing a different number. It involves asking the borrower to walk through what's in the request, and letting them arrive at the real number themselves.

How it sounds

A contractor has come in asking for $750,000 for a business expansion.

> **Owner:** "We're thinking $750,000 for the expansion. That covers construction, the new equipment, and gives us some buffer."
>
> **Banker:** "Let's work through what's in that number, because I want to make sure we're building toward something that actually fits the business. Walk me through the components, what's in the $750,000?"
>
> **Owner:** "Construction is probably $380,000. Equipment is $210,000. The rest is just extra, just in case."
>
> **Banker:** "So the known needs are $590,000. The $160,000 is a contingency. Is the construction number based on actual bids or an estimate at this point?"
>
> **Owner:** "Estimate. We haven't gone out for bids yet."

Banker: "That's useful to know, because it affects how we structure the contingency. Here's my concern with carrying $160,000 in undefined buffer: debt that doesn't have a clear purpose tends to stay on the books longer than it should. The monthly payments are higher, and during your ramp-up period when cash is tightest, you're servicing debt on money you may not have needed."

Owner: "But what if construction comes in over?"

Banker: "Great question, what's your best estimate of how much it could come in over?"

Owner: "I don't know. Maybe 10 or 15 percent."

Banker: "Okay, so 15% of $380,000 is about $57,000. That's a very different number than $160,000. What I'd recommend is going out for bids, getting a fixed-price contract if you can, and then structuring a realistic contingency based on the actual bid, something in the $50,000–70,000 range rather than an open-ended buffer. That way we're financing a real project, not a project plus a cushion."

Owner: "What if it comes in even higher?"

Banker: "Then we'd have a conversation at that point, with real numbers. A construction overrun with documented bids and a reason is a very manageable conversation. 'We borrowed $160,000 more than we needed just in case' is a harder one. I'd rather build toward the first scenario."

> **What happened here:** The borrower never heard "we won't do $750,000." The banker asked what was in the number, the borrower named the components, and the conversation shifted to whether $160,000 in undefined buffer made structural sense. By the end the borrower is thinking about getting real bids and sizing the contingency to actual risk, not defending the original ask.

The principle

Decompose before you decline. Most oversized requests contain a real need and a cushion. Separating them with the borrower's participation produces a better outcome than a flat refusal. The borrower feels heard. The structure improves. And you haven't made the borrower feel accused of asking for too much, you've helped them build toward something more defensible.

Conversation Five: Explaining a Personal Guarantee

The deal requires a personal guarantee. The borrower is resistant, they feel like they're being asked to put their personal assets on the line for a business decision, and the resistance is coming from a real place, not just a misunderstanding.

What most bankers do wrong

Explaining it as a bank requirement ("we require this on all commercial loans") or as bank protection ("it reduces our risk"). Both framings are accurate and both create resistance because they make the guarantee feel like something being done to the borrower for the bank's benefit.

The harder version of this conversation is when a borrower has a specific objection, a spouse who won't sign, a prior experience with a guarantee that went badly, or a genuine philosophical position about separating business and personal liability. Those objections deserve direct engagement, not a reframe that sidesteps them.

How it sounds

A business owner buying a commercial property has been told both she and her spouse need to sign a personal guarantee. She's come back with pushback from her spouse.

> **Owner:** "My husband won't sign. He says his name is not on the business and he doesn't want his personal assets at risk for a business decision."

Banker: "I understand that, and I want to give you a real answer rather than just telling you it's required. Can I ask a couple of questions first?"

Owner: "Sure."

Banker: "Is the property you're purchasing marital property, meaning you'd both be on the title?"

Owner: "Yes. We'd own it together."

Banker: "Then here's the honest situation. If his name is on the title and he's not on the guarantee, the bank has a secured interest in property he co-owns but no personal commitment from him to work through problems if they arise. From the bank's perspective, that's a gap. His interest in the outcome is real, it's in the title, but his commitment to the loan isn't. That asymmetry is what makes the guarantee necessary here."

Owner: "He's worried about what happens if the business fails and we lose the property and everything else."

Banker: "That's a legitimate concern and I don't want to dismiss it. Let me explain what a guarantee actually means in practice, because I think there's some fear in that scenario that isn't quite accurate."

Banker: "A personal guarantee means that if the business can't repay the loan, the bank can look to your personal assets. In most cases, and especially in owner-occupied real estate, the bank's first action is to work out a solution with the borrower, because foreclosure is expensive and slow. Guarantees are almost never the first move. They're the last resort. The bank wants this to perform, that's true whether he signs or not."

Owner: "Can you do the loan without his signature?"

Banker: "That's a question for credit, and I want to be honest with you: if he's on the title, they'll likely require his signature. But let me find out specifically what's possible and come back to you with a real answer rather than a maybe."

> **What happened here:** The borrower had a real objection from a real person, not just a vague discomfort. The banker asked clarifying questions, gave an honest explanation of why the guarantee was necessary in this specific situation, addressed the fear directly, and ended honestly about what credit would likely require rather than promising flexibility that might not exist.
>
> **Watch out:** Don't promise flexibility on guarantees that credit hasn't authorized. "I'll see what I can do" is worse than "I don't know yet but I'll find out."

The principle

Guarantees feel personal because they are personal. The emotional dimension is real and deserves direct acknowledgment. But emotional engagement doesn't mean softening the requirement, it means explaining it honestly and specifically. An owner who understands why the guarantee exists in their specific deal is more likely to accept it than one who's been given a policy explanation.

Conversation Six: Delivering a "Not Yet"

The deal isn't ready, not because the borrower is a poor credit, but because timing, cash flow stability, or structural gaps make it premature. You need to say no without saying never, and you need to hold that position when the borrower pushes back.

What most bankers do wrong

Three failures: vague deflection ("we'd need to see more history"), premature closure ("we can't approve this"), or false hope ("let's keep talking and see what happens"). All three leave the borrower without the specific information they need to actually move forward. The most common failure in this conversation isn't cruelty, it's imprecision.

The harder version is when the borrower argues that the timing is fine, they believe the business is ready even when the numbers suggest otherwise. Holding a "not yet" against a motivated, optimistic borrower requires a clear framework for what "ready" actually means. Without that, the conversation becomes a negotiation about opinions rather than a discussion about specific conditions.

How it sounds

A restaurant owner wants to finance a second location. Revenue has grown 28% in the past year but the business is 26 months old and the first location had a difficult first year.

> **Owner:** "I know you have some concerns, but I really think we're ready. Look at the last six months, everything is trending up."
>
> **Banker:** "I've looked carefully at the last six months, and you're right that the trend is positive. I want to be direct with you about why I'm still cautious, because I think you deserve a real explanation."
>
> **Owner:** "Okay."
>
> **Banker:** "The business is 26 months old. Your first twelve months were difficult, you told me yourself that you almost closed at month eight. The last fourteen months have been strong. What I can't tell yet is whether the strength is durable or whether it reflects a recovery from the difficult early period. A loan for a second location built on fourteen months of good performance, against a backdrop of twelve months of near-failure, is a loan that depends on the good period continuing. That's more fragility than I want to build into your structure."
>
> **Owner:** "But I've solved the problems that caused the early struggle. I changed suppliers, I changed my kitchen manager. It's genuinely different now."
>
> **Banker:** "I believe you. And those are real changes. Here's what I need to see to feel confident: two more quarters of financials that show the current margins holding, not just revenue growth, but profitability, and I'd want your line of credit to be below 30% utilization consistently, not just occasionally. Right now it's been above 70% for most of the last year."

Owner: "That's another six months. The location I want won't be available."

Banker: "That may be true, and I understand that's a real cost. But let me ask you a different question: if you opened a second location today and the first location had a difficult stretch, not a crisis, just a hard quarter, would the combined cash flow support both operations?"

Owner: "Probably not at the same time."

Banker: "That's the answer I needed you to say. Because that's the scenario I'm building structure for, not the best-case one. I'd rather you miss this space and be ready for the next one than take this space and have one difficult quarter threaten both locations."

Owner: "What exactly do I need to show you to change your answer?"

Banker: "Three things. Two full quarters with net margin above 12%, you're at 9% now. Line utilization below 30% for 60 consecutive days. And I'd want to talk through the transition plan for the new location, who runs it while you're still needed at location one. I'll check in with you at the 90-day mark regardless of where things stand."

> **What happened here:** The borrower pushed back twice, first arguing that they'd solved the problems, then raising the cost of the delay. The banker acknowledged both without conceding the position. The key moment is when the banker asked the scenario question ("if location one had a difficult quarter") and the owner answered honestly. That answer, "probably not", became the basis for why the "not yet" is correct, coming from the borrower rather than the banker.

The principle

A "not yet" without specific conditions is a soft decline that helps no one. Name the conditions. Make them measurable. Set a check-in date. And when the borrower argues that they're ready, ask them the scenario question: "if something difficult happened at the existing business while you were opening the new one, would the combined structure survive?" Their honest answer to that question is usually more persuasive than any analysis you can present.

Conversation Seven: Handling a Borrower Who Pushes Back on Structure

You've presented a structure. The borrower doesn't like one of the terms, the amortization is too short, the reporting feels intrusive, the covenant seems punitive. They're pushing back and the pushback has some emotional heat behind it.

What most bankers do wrong

Two failures. The first is caving: adjusting the structure to resolve the emotional pressure without a structural reason to do so. This creates a worse deal, signals that terms are negotiable on the basis of tone rather than substance, and sets a precedent for the rest of the relationship. The second is dismissal: holding firm with a policy explanation that makes the borrower feel unheard.

The productive path requires distinguishing between two types of pushback. One is emotional: the borrower doesn't like the term and is expressing that. The other is substantive: the borrower has a specific reason why the term doesn't fit their business. The first deserves acknowledgment. The second deserves a real conversation. Knowing which one you're in changes how you respond.

How it sounds

A manufacturing business owner has just received the term sheet. He's on the phone and clearly frustrated about the financial reporting covenant.

> **Owner:** "I've been in business for nineteen years and I've never had a bank ask for quarterly financials. This feels like you don't trust us."

Banker: "I hear that, and I want to explain where it's coming from rather than just telling you it's standard. Can I ask you a question first?"

Owner: "Sure."

Banker: "In the last five years, has your business ever had a quarter where cash flow came in significantly below what you expected at the start of that quarter?"

Owner: "Yeah. COVID hit us hard in 2020. And we had a supplier issue in 2022 that cost us about $180,000 in canceled orders."

Banker: "So twice in five years, external events created material cash flow impact on short notice. Quarterly reporting exists so that if something like that happens while this loan is outstanding, we know about it early enough to be helpful rather than reactive. Annual reporting means we might not know for twelve months that something changed. By then, options are limited."

Owner: "I understand the logic. But quarterly feels like a lot of work."

Banker: "I want to be honest about what it actually requires. We're asking for your internal P&L and balance sheet, not a full audit, not a compiled statement. Most businesses with a bookkeeper have this available within a couple of weeks of quarter-end. Is the quarterly cadence the issue, or is the format?"

Owner: "Honestly? My accountant charges me every time I ask for anything. It's the cost I'm worried about."

Banker: "Okay, that's a real and specific concern, and it's different from the reporting itself. Let me find out whether internal financials prepared by your bookkeeper satisfy the requirement, that's a very different cost conversation than your CPA preparing a compiled statement. I'll come back to you with a clear answer."

> **What happened here:** The borrower's initial pushback was emotional ("don't trust us") but his real concern turned out to be cost, not frequency. The banker didn't

> surface that by defending the covenant, they surfaced it by asking a question that made the borrower's actual concern visible. The covenant didn't change. The conversation became about how to satisfy it practically rather than whether it existed.
>
> **Watch out:** If a borrower's pushback on a term turns out to be substantive, they have a real operational reason why that term doesn't fit their business, bring it back to credit as a structural question, not as advocacy. "The borrower doesn't like this" is not a structural argument. "Here's why this covenant doesn't match how this business actually operates" sometimes is.

The principle

Distinguish emotional pushback from substantive pushback before responding to either. Acknowledge the emotion without conceding the structure. Ask what specifically isn't working. The borrower's real concern is almost always more specific than their opening objection, and a specific concern has a specific answer.

Conversation Eight: Responding to an Angry Decline

The deal has been declined. The borrower is angry, maybe they feel misled, maybe they think the decision is wrong, maybe they're directing frustration at you personally. You need to stay steady, be honest, and give them something useful to take away.

What most bankers do wrong

Three failures. Excessive apology: repeating "I'm sorry" multiple times, which signals the decision might be wrong and makes the banker seem unsteady. Hiding behind credit ("it was out of my hands"): which destroys trust and makes the banker seem powerless in their own institution. Overexplanation to justify: which shifts the conversation to defending the bank rather than helping the borrower.

The hardest version is when the borrower's anger is partly justified. Maybe the process took longer than it should have. Maybe signals were given that the deal was closer to approval than it was. In those cases, the banker needs to acknowledge what's true without capitulating on the decision itself, a distinction most bankers find genuinely difficult.

How it sounds

A borrower's acquisition loan was declined after six weeks in process. He's calling the banker and he's clearly upset.

> **Owner:** "Six weeks. I turned down another buyer for this business because I thought we were close. Now you're telling me no? I could have sold this differently."
>
> **Banker:** "I hear you, and I'm not going to tell you that frustration isn't warranted. Six weeks is a long time, and I want to be honest with you about what happened."
>
> **Owner:** "What happened is you wasted my time."
>
> **Banker:** "Here's what I can tell you honestly. When we started, I thought this deal had a path. The business fundamentals are real. What changed as we got deeper into the financials were two things I couldn't resolve with the seller's records. The last two years of tax returns show a pattern of owner distributions that reduced reported income below what the P&Ls were showing. And the customer list, when we looked at contract terms, three of the top five customers are month-to-month with no renewal commitment. Together, those two things created a repayment picture that credit couldn't get comfortable with."
>
> **Owner:** "Why didn't you tell me that three weeks ago?"
>
> **Banker:** "The tax return issue surfaced in week four when the seller's CPA finally got us the amended returns. The customer contract review happened in week five. I should have flagged the possibility of those issues earlier as risks to timeline rather than waiting until we had answers. That's a fair criticism."
>
> **Owner:** "So what do I do now?"
>
> **Banker:** "I'll tell you exactly what I'd want to see if you come back to this deal or a similar one. The tax return issue needs to be cleaned up, the seller needs to be able to show that the

distributions were legitimate and that reported income matches actual business performance. The customer concentration issue needs a structural answer, either multiyear contract commitments from those top five, or you need to price the acquisition differently to account for the revenue risk. Neither of those things is impossible. They just weren't in place."

Owner: "And if I find another buyer who doesn't care about those things?"

Banker: "That's your call. But I'd tell you that any lender who looks carefully at the tax returns and the customer contracts will find the same things we found. If someone doesn't ask, you should ask why."

> **What happened here:** The banker acknowledged what was legitimately frustrating, the timeline was long and the issues surfaced late. They didn't hide behind process or credit. They named the specific issues clearly, gave the borrower an honest path forward, and ended with a line that positions them as a candid advisor rather than an obstacle. The relationship may not survive this conversation intact, but it has a better chance than it would with an apology and a shrug.

The principle

A well-handled decline is one of the most trust-building moments in a banking relationship, not because the borrower is happy, but because honesty in a hard moment is rarer than most people expect. Acknowledge what's legitimate in the frustration. Name the specific issues. Give the borrower something actionable to take away. Don't apologize for the decision. And if you made a process mistake, own it directly and specifically, not as a general apology, but as a named acknowledgment of what should have happened differently.

Quick Reference: Language That Works and Language That Doesn't

The words you choose matter more than most bankers realize. Here are the most common language traps, and what to say instead.

Avoid this…	Try this instead…
"Credit requires this."	"This is how the structure works, and here's why it matters for your business."
"I'll see what I can do."	"Here's what I think is realistic, and here's why."
"It was out of my hands."	"I want to explain what drove the decision."
"We need to see more history."	"Here are the three specific things that need to change."
"The DSCR doesn't support it."	"The cash flow doesn't comfortably cover the payment based on what you've shown me."
"I wish I could do more."	"Here's what I can do, and why I think it's the right structure."
"Let's keep talking and see."	"Here's what ready looks like. Let's set a date to reconnect."
"That's just how we do it."	"This exists for a specific reason, let me explain it."

"You don't qualify."	"The structure doesn't fit where the business is right now."
"I'm sorry about the decision."	"I understand the frustration. Let me explain exactly what happened."
"Can you give me a few days to look into it?"	"I'll have a specific answer for you by [date]."

A Final Thought on Conversation

Commercial lending conversations are not negotiations. They're not performances. At their best, they're collaborative problem-solving, two people working together to figure out whether a loan makes sense and what it should look like.

The eight scenarios in this guide are not the only difficult conversations you'll have. They're demonstrations of an approach: be specific, stay honest, hold the structure when the structure is right, and acknowledge what's legitimate in the borrower's concern before explaining why it doesn't change the answer.

The most important thing to notice in every worked example is not what the banker says. It's what the banker asks. Good commercial conversations are driven by questions, not explanations. The banker who asks the right question at the right moment almost always gets a better outcome than the one who knows what to say.

The borrower who trusts you is the one who heard hard things from you and felt respected anyway. That's built in conversation, one honest exchange at a t

Appendix C: Front-End Lending Reference Guide

The following ten reference pages are designed to be used, not just read. Print them, keep them open during calls, share them with your team. Each one distills a core concept from the book into something you can reach for in the moment.

Reference Page 1

The Front-End Lending Framework

Use this before every commercial conversation

Before any deal moves forward, answer all five questions clearly and in plain language. If the answers are fuzzy, the deal isn't ready.

1. **What is really happening inside this business?** Not the pitch, the operating reality.
2. **Why does this business need debt right now?** Timing matters as much as purpose.
3. **How will this loan be repaid under normal conditions?** Not best-case conditions.
4. **What happens if things don't go as planned?** Structure exists for this moment.
5. **Does the structure fit the risk?** Or is one element doing too much work?

> ***If you can't answer all five in plain language, the deal isn't ready.***

Reference Page 2

Consumer to Commercial Translation Guide

Use this to rewire your thinking

Consumer Lending	Commercial Lending
Product selection	Problem diagnosis
Credit score	Cash flow + behavior
Debt-to-income	Repayment capacity
Collateral value	Secondary protection
Approval	Ongoing relationship
One-time decision	Continuous monitoring

> *Consumer lending qualifies borrowers. Commercial lending structures risk.*

Reference Page 3

Front-End Deal Flow

Use this to stay oriented

Most outcomes are decided by Step 4. The steps before it create the conditions. The steps after it confirm them.

6. **Conversation** (raw request, treat it as a starting point, not a proposal)
7. **Discovery** (what's really happening inside the business)
8. **Reframing** (what the business actually needs, translated back to the borrower)
9. **Structuring** (shape risk into something workable, this is where outcomes are decided)
10. **Pressure-testing** (where could this break? fix it now, not later)
11. **Credit review** (a checkpoint, not a verdict)
12. **Communicate the outcome** (clearly, regardless of the result)
13. **Relationship management** (the loan is the beginning, not the end)

> ***The front end is the cheapest place to fix a problem. Take advantage of it.***

Reference Page 4

Structure Cheat Sheet

Use this when shaping deals

Element	What It's Really Doing
Amount	Solve the problem, not the wish. Smaller is often stronger.
Term	Match the life of the need. Use term intentionally, not conveniently.
Amortization	How fast risk burns off. Balances sustainability with accountability.
Repayment source	Cash flow, not hope. If this sentence is fuzzy, the structure is too.
Collateral	Reduces loss, does not create repayment. Protection, not permission.
Guarantees	Align behavior, not fix structure. Should reinforce, not replace.
Monitoring	Catch problems early. More volatility = more structure needed.

> *If one element is doing all the work, structure is off.*

Reference Page 5

Lines vs. Terms: Quick Decision Guide

Use this to avoid the most common mistake

Lines of Credit	Term Loans
USE WHEN:	**USE WHEN:**
• The need is temporary • Cash cycles repeat • Balances should rise and fall	• Financing something with a life • The benefit lasts longer than a cycle • Repayment should shrink risk over time
RED FLAGS:	**RED FLAGS:**
• Always fully drawn • Funding long-term needs • Never pays down	• Funding operating losses • Repayment depends on refinancing • "This will buy us time"

> ***Lines solve cycles. Terms solve longevity. Combinations solve complexity.***

Reference Page 6

Common Front-End Warning Signs

Use this to slow things down early

A single warning sign rarely means much. A cluster of them usually does. These are not decline signals, they are structure signals.

- Urgency without a clear explanation
- Vague use of proceeds
- Repayment depends on "next year"
- Permanent use of temporary tools (lines that never pay down)
- Resistance to basic questions
- Guarantees doing all the work
- "This is how we've always done it"
- One loan trying to fix everything at once
- Borrower focused only on approval, not fit
- You feel uneasy, but can't explain why

> ***Warning signs are not reasons to stop. They are reasons to ask better questions.***

Reference Page 7

How to Explain Structure

Use this to build trust without weakening discipline

Borrowers don't need to love structure. They need to understand it. Language matters.

Instead of saying…	Try this…
"Credit requires this"	"This helps us manage risk early."
"We need protection"	"This gives us room if things change."
"These are covenants"	"These are check-in points."
"You don't qualify"	"The structure doesn't fit yet."
"This was declined"	"The timing isn't right today."
"This is a covenant breach"	"Let's talk about what changed."

> ***Explain why before what. Tie structure to the borrower's own goals.***

Reference Page 8

When the Right Answer Is "Not Yet"

Use this to protect relationships

"Not yet" is one of the most powerful things a banker can say, and one of the hardest. Used well, it preserves trust, prevents regret, and often leads to better deals later.

"Not yet" is usually the right answer when:

- Cash flow is improving but not yet stable
- Growth hasn't shown up in the numbers yet
- Structure would rely on hope rather than cash flow
- Timing creates pressure the business isn't ready to carry

A good "not yet" conversation includes:

- What specifically would need to change
- What to watch for in the meantime
- When to revisit, and what that conversation looks like

> ***Waiting is a form of structure. Bankers who understand this don't feel pressure to force outcomes that aren't ready.***

Reference Page 9

The Banker's Self-Check

Use this before sending anything to credit

Ask yourself these five questions before any deal moves forward. If the answers feel fuzzy, pause.

- **What question will credit ask first?** Answer it before they have to.
- **Where could this break?** Name it specifically, then address it.
- **What am I assuming?** Assumptions that haven't been tested are risks that haven't been managed.
- **What would I wish I had asked later?** Ask it now.
- **Would I be surprised if this struggled?** If yes, something still needs work.

> ***The front-end self-check isn't about doubt. It's about discipline.***

Reference Page 10

The One Question That Never Fails

Use this when stuck

When you're unsure whether a structure is right, when a deal feels off but you can't explain why, when you're about to move forward but something is nagging, ask this:

> ***If this loan were already outstanding, how would it feel on the borrower's worst month, not their best one?***

Then listen to your honest answer.

Your answer is...	That means...
"Manageable but firm"	You're probably close. Keep going.
"Crushing"	Restructure. The payment burden is too high.
"Irrelevant"	Rethink the need. This loan may not be solving the right problem.
"I'm not sure"	That's the answer. Go back and do more discovery.

> ***Good lending doesn't eliminate risk. It eliminates surprise.***

The Discipline of Banking

Banking is often described as a business of products, policies, and transactions. In reality, it is a business of judgment.

Every day, bankers help members make financial decisions, design loans that must work over time, monitor risk as conditions change, and lead institutions through uncertainty. When judgment is inconsistent, risk accumulates quietly. When judgment is disciplined, institutions become resilient.

The Discipline of Banking exists to clarify that judgment.

Each book focuses on one discipline required for strong financial institutions: guiding members toward sound decisions, structuring credit carefully, recognizing risk before it becomes visible, forming capable leaders, and stewarding institutions with responsibility.

These disciplines are simple, but they are not automatic. They must be practiced intentionally across the organization.

Good banking is not a moment of approval or a single transaction.

It is a continuous act of judgment.

This Book's Role in the Discipline of Banking

The Discipline of Banking describes a set of core disciplines that determine whether financial institutions perform reliably over time. Each book in the series examines one discipline at the point where judgment enters the system and begins to compound.

Loan by Design ™ focuses on the discipline of **commercial loan structure**.

Before credit policy is applied, before underwriting is performed, and long before a loan is monitored or managed, a more fundamental decision is made: whether a loan should exist at all, and, if it should, how it must be structured to endure.

That decision is rarely made in a committee room. It is made at the front end, in conversation, as a banker listens to a business owner describe a need and translates that need into structure. This is where risk is either shaped deliberately or embedded quietly into the loan from the start.

When loans are built with clear purpose, realistic repayment, and structure that anticipates how a business actually operates, they tend to perform quietly over time. When structure is vague, oversized, or doing work it was never designed to do, problems are not avoided, they are merely postponed.

This book explains how experienced bankers think at that front end. It is not a guide to approval mechanics or policy interpretation. It is a study of the judgment required to design credit that fits the business, respects risk and holds up long after the deal is closed.

The Discipline of Banking

For Retail Bankers	**The Advice-Based Banker ™** The Discipline of Member Guidance in Credit Unions
For Commercial Lenders	**Loan By Design ™** The Discipline of Loan Structure **The Cash Discipline ™** The Discipline of Operating Cash
For Commercial Loan	**The Quiet Risk Model ™** The Discipline of Credit Stewardship in Commercial Lending
For High Performing Leaders	**The Assembled Leader ™** The Discipline of Leadership Formation in Regulated Industries
For Executive Teams	**The Leadership Tax ™** The Discipline of Capacity Stewardship
For Everyone	**Money In. Money Out. Risk Stays.** How Credit Unions Work, From the Inside

About the Author

Chad W. Maze spent the first part of his career doing commercial lending the way most people learn it, on the job, deal by deal, figuring out through trial and experience what the training hadn't quite covered. He worked with small businesses, midsize companies, real estate owners, and first-generation entrepreneurs. Some of those deals were straightforward. Some were not. All of them taught him something.

What he kept noticing, across years of front-end lending work, was a consistent gap. The bankers around him who struggled weren't struggling because they lacked intelligence or effort. They were struggling because no one had ever given them a framework for how to *think* about commercial lending at the front end, before the numbers, before the credit memo, before the moment when most of the outcome had already been determined.

Eventually he moved out of the banker's seat and into the work of developing bankers, coaching, training, and building curriculum for institutions trying to bring consumer and branch lenders into commercial roles. That transition put him in front of hundreds of bankers at different stages of the same journey. The framework in this book is what emerged from all of it: the principles he found himself teaching over and over, distilled into a form that could travel without him in the room.

The borrowers in his background range from sole proprietors running tight operations on thin margins to multilocation businesses managing growth faster than their cash flow could comfortably support to multibillion-dollar public names. He has worked on equipment deals and acquisition financing, owner-occupied real estate and working capital lines, SBA transactions and conventional structures. He has seen deals that looked clean fall apart and deals that looked difficult come together, almost always because of what happened or didn't happen at the front end.

His work with financial institutions has taken him across community banks, regional banks, and credit unions at various stages of building or rebuilding their commercial lending practices. The common thread in all of it: the technical knowledge is rarely the gap. The front-end thinking is.

This book is not the one Chad wished he had when he started. He didn't know enough then to know what he was missing. It's the book he wishes he could have handed to every banker he watched struggle, the capable ones, the well-intentioned ones, the ones who were doing their best with an incomplete map.

Commercial lending is a craft. It can be taught. That conviction is the reason this book exists.

www.ingramcontent.com/pod-product-compliance
Lightning Source LLC
LaVergne TN
LVHW011127300926
849160LV00008B/538
* 9 7 9 8 9 9 5 6 3 5 9 6 3 *